EFFECTIVE WORKING with RURAL COMMUNITIES

Seizing the Opportunities

James Garo Derounian

PACKARD PUBLISHING LIMITED
CHICHESTER

EFFECTIVE WORKING WITH RURAL COMMUNITIES

© James Garo Derounian.

Individual chapters also © Malcolm Moseley,
Elisabeth Skinner, and Rhys Taylor, as indicated in the text.

First published in 1998 by Packard Publishing Limited,
Forum House, Stirling Road, Chichester, West Sussex PO19 2EN.

ISBN 1 85341 105 1 (hardback)
ISBN 1 85341 106 X (softback)

A CIP record for this book is available from the British Library.

Frontispiece cartoon reproduced with kind permission of David Austin and NCVO.

Front-cover photograph of a Yorkshire village shop by S. Bean; back-cover photograph of Cloune Community Learning Opportunity Centre by T. Clayton; both copyright Rural Development Commission.

Typeset by The Phoenix Setting Company, Portsmouth, Hampshire.

Printed and bound in the United Kingdom by
RPM Reprographics, Chichester, West Sussex.

EFFECTIVE WORKING WITH RURAL COMMUNITIES
Seizing the Opportunities

Rural community development is the process of deliberate change engineered at local level. This book gives practical advice about achieving constructive change for practitioners working in the British countryside: social and community workers, church workers, health professionals, teachers, doctors, local and national government agencies, voluntary sector bodies such as Citizens Advice Bureaux and community councils, and anyone else committed to collaborative action. Many students during their training in Rural Studies in higher or adult education will find pointers to a worthwhile career in the countryside. Parish councillors and villagers themselves will be helped by this book to understand the workings of their communities, to recognize who wields power in their localities and how to exert influence.

Contents

List of Tables

List of Figures

Dedication

For Linsey, Sam and Flora, with much love.

And to all those that I love and who are now in the 'shadows'
or perhaps in the light; especially Mum, Auntie Haines and
my dear friend Nick Collin, who I think of often.

Acknowledgements

And three apples fell from Heaven:
one for the teller of the story . . . and one for him who read it.

(Three Apples Fell From Heaven, *Armenian Folk Tales*,
edited by Mischa Kudian, 1969)

The above quote has particular meaning for me as an Englishman of Armenian extraction: it expresses the desire that a book should be valuable to the author and reader alike. I hope this proves true for you in relation to the present text.

My thanks go to the following people for their help during the preparation of this book: Jonathan Brown, Mark Callan, David Clark for suggestions about the text, Bengt Dahlgren, Gordon Daly, Gwen Davis from Buckinghamshire Council for Voluntary Service, Gem Duncan from Age Concern, Leominster, Iain Elkington, Jordi Falgarona, Ann Fitzpatrick, Phil Gravestock for extensive proof-reading, Neil Greenhalf, Laurie Howes, Fran Huckle and ACRE's *Rural Digest*, Ro Lyon, Caro McIntosh, Lisa Morris, Ian Nelson, Michael Packard for his encouragement, Hannah Reynolds, Julie Ryan, Alister Scott, Tim Shaw of Newcastle University, David Smith, Lyn Thompson in Swindon, Lyn Turner and Alan Baty from Tynedale Council, Penny Whitehead, and Drs John, Nubar and Zabelle Derounian.

I would also like to thank the following artists, photographers and organizations for permission to reproduce their illustrations: David Austin and NCVO for the frontispiece cartoon; Bamberton, British Columbia, for its 'code': Chris Chapman for his photograph of drystone walling on Dartmoor; The Citizens' Charter Unit for the cartoon from its Rural Services Checklist; the Leader 1 Observatory, AEIDL, Brussels, for the map and details of Portuguese Leader 1 areas; Mandy Lockley for unearthing the frontispiece cartoon; Long Ashton Parish Appraisal Committee for drawings from its publication; Northamptonshire ACRE for extracts from its Parish 2000 leaflet; PUNCH Magazine for the 1863 cartoon of the Pig and the Peasant; Rural Action for the Environment for its 1992 Commitment Statement; the Rural Development Commission Library for its 1995 map of the English Development Areas and the cover photographs; Elisabeth Skinner for the photographs of Sheepscombe from her collection; and Simon Stern and the Inkshed for the satirical view of parish councils which first appeared in *Country Life*.

Last but not least, special thanks go to Malcolm Moseley (Chapters 7 and 10), Elisabeth Skinner (Chapter 6) and Rhys Taylor (Chapter 8) as contributory authors, and also for comments on the book. Elisabeth deserves particular mention for her rigorous and constructive comments on all the draft chapters; also to the 1995, 6 and 7 classes of Local Policy and Countryside Planning students at Cheltenham who had no choice but constructively to criticize draft chapters; and to Simon Silvester and Elizabeth Young for use of material from their final year undergraduate dissertations.

James Derounian
Cheltenham, 1997

Preface

Improving the quality of life in the countryside
starts with local people and local initiative.

At last there is official recognition of the sense and power of community-based rural action! In fact the idea of development based on community comment and preference is beginning to surface in various contemporary discussions, particularly in relation to translating sustainability into practice. English Nature (1994) advocates the benefits of "going beyond consultation and seeking the active participation of groups and organisations in drawing up plans and strategies and in implementing and monitoring them".

Effective Working, seeks to inform this groundswell of opinion favouring locally generated solutions. The book is aimed chiefly at practitioners working in the British countryside: social and community workers, health professionals, teachers, doctors, local and national government agencies, voluntary sector bodies such as Citizens Advice Bureaux and Community Councils, and anyone else committed to collaborative action. The book will also help villagers themselves to understand the workings of their communities (Chapters 1 and 6), recognize who wields power in their localities and how to exert influence (Chapters 2 and 3), as well as give details of the practical development 'tools' that can be deployed to bring about constructive change (Chapters 5 and 7).

The need for co-operation between agencies and rural communities was recognized in responses to central Government when organizations sought to influence the content of the 1995 White Paper on the English Countryside. The Royal Town Planning Institute (RTPI), for example, sought a "rural policy . . . to create a more integrated approach at all levels – from the European Community to the individual . . ." (RTPI, 1995).

The new emphasis on active community involvement in decision-making is, perhaps, most cogently expressed by the pan-European Council for the Village and Small Town (ECOVAST) in its 1994 *Strategy for Rural Europe* which seeks "a balance, and mutual support, between people and the environment. We look for integrated action between different arms of government, and between government and local people. We expect the local people to be consulted and involved". This implies much more than a passive exercise in hearing, but rather an active process of listening and acting accordingly. It steps beyond national government planning guidance (PPG12), which sought to make it "easier for people to be involved in the planning process", but made no promises to act on locally-articulated preferences (Department of the Environment, 1992).

Effective Working arises from continuing work with rural communities. My motivation in organizing the book is to broadcast ideas for good practice and to foster networking in which "relationships and contacts between people or organisations are established, nurtured and utilised for mutual benefit" (Gilchrist, 1995).

I have been influenced by the late Professor Gerald Wibberley, who lectured to me at London University (Wye College) in the late 1970s. He emphasized the importance of people in the countryside and how hard country living can often be. I have become increasingly concerned to pull back the lace curtain obscuring the view of contemporary rural life, and to reveal 'Another Country' (Derounian, 1993).

During my time in Devon (with the voluntary sector Community Council) and in Northumberland (via a local authority-led Rural Development Programme), I have had the privilege to work alongside local people in retaining village schools, opening shops, restoring derelict properties to new uses, and in helping residents determine local preferences through community appraisals. It has been a salutary experience to find so many people from very different backgrounds who share a strong belief in themselves, their communities and their ability to make a difference.

This book charts the parameters of rural community development practice and its overall objective is to inform professionals in the field, and also villagers, as to how they can work effectively together. Although there is a measure of theory, this publication is meant to be a practical tool to foster community action and greater self-confidence amongst villagers; it deliberately does not, to any significant extent, retread familiar themes in contemporary rural life – affordable housing, preservation versus economic development, declining service provision or rural deprivation. Those issues only surface as they influence the practice of rural community development. What the book does attempt is to give practical expression to current, topical discussions on sustainability, the integration of social, economic and conservation activities, as well as ways of engendering grassroots approaches to regeneration.

With typical directness Michael Dower, recent Director of the Government's Countryside Commission, has gone to the heart of the matter: "Local people often have a far better feel for what is appropriate and sustainable in their area than do governments. Moreover it is their future . . . in considering the means for action, we (speaking on behalf of ECOVAST) therefore place a first focus on the views and wishes, the resources and energies, of local people in each place. The challenge is to link their views and resources to those of governments at all levels" (1995).

Effective Working seeks to forge and strengthen that link between local aspirations and willing and able external agencies. I hope it avoids presenting obvious and well-known ideas and dressing them up "in fancy conceptual language – a form of intellectual obfuscation of interpretation designed to appeal to restricted elite audiences who shared the common code of jargonised text" (Cloke, 1994). While the primary focus is on rural England the book does draw on examples from Wales, Scotland, Ireland, Scandinavia and mainland Europe.

The book falls into two sections: the first three chapters set down the context for rural community development in England during the late 1990s. Chapter 1 explores the nature of rural lifestyles, how different groups coexist and relate to each other within rural communities. Chapter 2 then identifies the internal 'players' and structures within villages – the Parish Council, WI, etc. Chapter 3 highlights the external players – the local authorities, QUANGOs and so on – and mechanisms that affect individual settlements.

Section two moves on to look at the practical delivery of rural community development. Chapter 4 discusses key themes in rural development – ownership, integration and networking among others. Chapter 5 recognizes the potential and limitations of certain tools used in fostering community development; these include newsletters, patchwork and adult education. Five examples then follow, illustrating respectively, a locality-based approach, the use of parish appraisals, environmental action, the role of a particular resource (the village school), and the impact of central and European government (EU) initiatives on rural development. Chapter 6, written by Elisabeth Skinner, dissects the small Cotswold community of Sheepscombe and seeks to explain how it functions. Chapter 7 by Malcolm Moseley, discusses Village Appraisals and their practical outcomes. Chapter 8 by Rhys Taylor critically analyses the history, operation, evaluation and future work of the national Rural Action for the Environment initiative and concentrates on one, early, attempt to make practical sense of sustainability. Chapter 9 recognizes the possibilities for village schools to act as engines of community development. The last case study, Chapter 10, written again by Malcolm Moseley, focuses on community development initiatives at home and abroad, and in particular on English Rural Development Programmes (RDPs) and EU LEADER projects. The final chapter looks to the future of rural community development, and paints two contrasting pictures. A full bibliography and index complete the book.

James Derounian

Chapter 1

Rural Lifestyles

Lifestyles in Rural England is the title of a 1994 report from the Government's Rural Development Commission (RDC). It exploded a number of popular myths about the countryside: some villagers expressed feelings of being left out or "marginalised in what they thought of as their own place, as others moved in and brought with them relative affluence, influence, different political and social ambitions, and even a different view of what rurality was all about" (Cloke *et al.*, 1994). Young people were portrayed as struggling to enter the housing market; lack of public transport constituted a major stumbling block to gaining paid employment; and one in five households was classified as being in, or on the margins of, poverty, with the elderly most likely to feel the cold blast of penury.

Non-agricultural employment accounted for between 76 and 95 per cent of the rural workforce and, according to the Lifestyles document, the grey economy is alive and well in the English countryside, with a significant number of people holding down second jobs (so-called 'foreigners') while formally unemployed. Of particular relevance and concern to rural development is the impact of increasing numbers of women (re)entering the workforce, which means that they are "less able to devote time to community work, and as a result some community institutions and practices were thought to be suffering" (Cloke *et al.*, 1994).

While a host of rural services – shops, pubs, schools – continue to decline in number, the Lifestyles survey pointed to a 'blind-spot', in which "the notion of deprivation was stigmatic for some respondents and 'out of sight, out of mind' for others" (Cloke *et al.*, 1994). The expectation of living in a close-knit community was variously perceived as either supportive or a "prying, gossiping intrusion", all of which highlights the fact that the 'rural community' does not exist! There is no homogenous lump that constitutes a village community.

This chapter, therefore, will look at the different groups that comprise 'the community', how they relate and at their impact, with differing needs and aspirations, on rural community development.

It was the rural sociologist Howard Newby who memorably coined the phrase 'two nations in one village' to illustrate the tensions between generally wealthier incomers and their relatively poor indigenous neighbours. This is not the only potential divide or distinction within the village, but the point must be to consider the village as a community of communities. The dimensions or boundaries of these discrete units are variously constructed. 1991 census data confirm the exodus of people from the cities to towns and villages: a process known as 'counterurbanization'. This trend is clearly shown in Table 1a.

Table 1a *Types of District*	**Population Movements 1981-1991** *Population (thousands)*	*Change 1981-1991 (%)*
Greater London		
Inner boroughs	–147	–5.9
Outer boroughs	–172	–4.1
Metropolitan districts		
Principal cities	–370	–8.7
Other districts	–372	–4.3
Non-metropolitan districts		
Large cities	–131	–3.7
Small cities	+11	+0.6
Industrial areas	–42	–0.6
New town districts	+133	+5.0
Resorts, ports and retirement areas	+174	+5.2
Urban and mixed urban/rural	+319	+3.3
Remoter, mainly rural	+366	+6.1

Source: Champion, 1991

Geographical or Spatial Differentiation

There was a row of council houses tacked on to the end of the street, their brick injuriously red against the cooler colours of the landscape. Most had corrugated iron shacks at the back in which chickens and rabbits were kept, and one had several cars in bits and pieces parked across the front garden. Almost all the older houses had been refurbished as commuter homes and retirement cottages: pink washed plaster, timbers exposed, roofs re-thatched. (Clarke, 1989)

Whether viewing a place through a car windscreen or walking village streets, settlements can be seen to comprise different communities through their configuration, physical layout and different architectural styles. A classic example of this can be seen in the way that council houses were originally sited at the edge of a village or herded into a compound or ghetto. At Fourstones near Hexham, for example, the council estate is set away from the pretty main street, as a free-standing community divorced from the rest of the village. In the small former Forestry Commission settlement of Byrness, Northumberland, owner occupiers are clearly identified by the new paintwork and home improvements; by contrast the state-owned properties tend to be in poorer repair. Kingham in Oxfordshire even names its council-house quarter as 'Canada', because the residents are seen to be apart or as foreigners, who might just as well come from across the Atlantic!

By contrast if you visit the archetypal Cotswold village of Stanton, you become aware of the influence of the Manor House or landed estate. Stanton has a unity of design which is immediately striking: honeyed stone cottages with undulating roofs. The same is true of the estate villages of Guiting Power in the south-west and Ford and Etal at the north-east corner of England. The country house is a deliberately conspicuous indicator of (former) wealth and power. You would not, for example, fail to be impressed by country 'piles' like Floors castle, home of the Duke of Roxburgh, or Ugbrooke, which the Devon peer Lord Chudleigh owns. The 'big house' makes a statement and sets its occupants physically and socially apart from the rest of humanity. In Charles Dickens' novel, *Hard Times*, the factory owner Gradgrind lives in a house well away from the sight and sounds of the industry which makes him wealthy: Coketown "had a black canal in it, and a river that ran purple with ill-smelling dye, and vast piles of building full of windows where there was a rattling and a trembling all day long . . ."

A latter-day example of conspicuous consumption comes in the form of second or holiday home ownership; and there are particular concentrations in areas of high landscape value, where planning constraints militate against house building as appears in the National Parks of England and Wales. The Parks attract second and holiday home ownership, often to the detriment of (local) people on low incomes who simply cannot compete in the housing market. This can unsurprisingly breed resentment, so that spatial distinctions spill over into social polarization. An extreme manifestation of this hostility has been the fire-bombing of English-owned properties in Wales, by the Sons of Glyndwr.

The implication for rural community development is that there must be thorough and careful interpretation of who is asking for what within a community. For example, the results of a parish appraisal might show a need for affordable housing within a particular community but there has to be an indication of **who** is asking and **where** they live. This information builds up a clear picture of **need** as distinct from **demand**. If an appraisal represents the views of people from several different settlements within the same parish, it could be that those from one village are requesting play facilities, parking restrictions and no new housing in a location where they do not live!

Social Differentiation

There can be social differentiation, within rural communities. Disputes and distinctions between incomers and indigenous residents provide the obvious expression of that difference. Joyce Halliday at Exeter University (1991) noted that many migrants to Devon in the 1990s were not only new to the county but, "in many instances, new to the countryside" as well. And it is from that starting point that cultural attitudes can be seen as a source of division within rural communities. NIMBYism ('not in my back yard') is the classic attitude of 'new villagers' to development; and it is ironical that people buy into what they see as a preferable model of community, only to start a retrogressive process that, if taken to its ultimate conclusion, will destroy the very thing that attracted them in the first place. Nevertheless there are those who argue that NIMBY responses at least demonstrate strong concern by (some) people for their surrounds.

There is a darker side to such behaviour. Boundary disputes and development proposals can trigger particular division and acrimony between, say, a local farmer selling off land for development and any 'new neighbours' whose Eden (and house prices) are threatened. There are commonplace but true stories based on different cultural expectations when incomers, looking for peace, quiet and nothing malodorous, experience heavy farm machinery droning through the harvest nights, and the shock of the nauseous smells from slurry and oilseed rape at unexpected times of the year. 'Corky the Cockerel' who lives in the Devon village of Stoke Cannon provides a true example of colliding tolerances. Corky crowed, as cocks do, and neighbours complained. The upshot was a court injunction restricting the hours that Corky was able to crow! At Woodbury, near Exmouth, where there is a fine parish church standing in a raised churchyard, the pealing of bells on a Sunday morning to summon the faithful has led to complaints about disturbing the peace!

Finally there is the story of a redundant smithy in one home counties' village that a blacksmith wanted to restore to working use. The planning application was strongly opposed by the commuting residents of the settlement, who formed a majority of the population, as being smelly, noisy, dirty and not in keeping with the tranquillity of the village! So there is, at one and the same time, a desire to

THE PIG AND THE PEASANT.

Peasant. "AH! I'D LIKE TO BE CARED VOR HALF AS WELL AS THEE BE!"

Figure 1.1   Rural deprivation – a hidden, but not a new phenomenon
(Reproduced with permission of Punch Ltd)

experience a 'genuine' rural community, but equally there is the 'temptation to preserve' their piece of heaven so that no changes erode it.

Bishop Anthony Russell, a government-appointed Rural Development Commissioner, wrote in 1986 suggesting why incomers and longer-standing residents display such different reactions to involvement and participation in village affairs and societies: he argued that activity is seen as a passport to acceptance for newcomers. By contrast Russell sees indigenous families as absorbing their sense of place by some passive process of osmosis, as if exposure over a long period of time, generations even, enables assimilation into the underlying knowledge of place, rather as blotting paper mops up water. It is interesting to see, in this respect, the way in which the surnames of reivers in Cumbria, Northumberland and the Scottish borders from centuries ago – Armstrong, Rutherford and Charlton – still commonly pop up in the contemporary telephone directories for those areas and attest to their historical roots. Russell's thesis is persuasive in giving sense to the way in which incomers are accused of 'taking over' the Women's Institute (WI) or parish council, and equally the reverse charge that longer-standing residents are fatalistic, apathetic and don't 'pull their weight'. But see Chapter 6, in relation to the village of Sheepscombe, to gain a subtler insight into the activities of more established and relatively recent arrivals to that community.

Other facets of social stratification include relative wealth as the overall impression of the countryside, an image that at once masks and denies the existence of poverty and deprivation. This view seems to be corroborated by the relatively high levels of car ownership in rural areas; although possession of a car is in fact both a cause and effect of disadvantage. It is an effect when poor service provision – few buses, or village shop closures – and the need to travel to work demand that a car is available; however, low rural wages combined with higher petrol costs plus maintenance mean that drivers can actually fall into a vicious circle, or poverty trap. Housing is the other big divider within rural communities, where restrictive planning policies, sale of council houses, early retirement, cultural expectations of 'a place in the country', and massive repopulation of the countryside have served to force prices out of the reach of younger, local, people on low incomes. These factors can lead quite understandably to frustration, anger and resentment, when people are forced out of their 'home' communities.

The danger is that vocal, articulate middle-class residents express themselves at the expense of a significant and silent minority. Public meetings, as an example, can be hijacked by vociferous **objectors**; and there would appear to be a stronger urge to **object** than to confirm or support ventures. Community development workers must be aware of the possibility of opinions and proposals that only reflect a partial viewpoint; also that they operate in ways that do not allow genuine access, involvement, and representative views to be collected. Different cultural perspectives and expectations can, therefore, play havoc with community dynamics: the rural lifestyles report (Cloke *et al.*, 1994), as already noted at the start of this chapter, demonstrated the existence of a thriving 'grey economy' in rural areas. On the southern tip of the isle of Arran, for example, there is a farmer who doubles as the lighthouse keeper, jobbing builder, bed and breakfast operator and occasional seaweed collector! So the cash economy and the stitching together of various part-time jobs in order to make a living, have been traditional in many rural areas. But for newcomers such behaviour can run close to tax or benefits evasion, and thereby give further cause for mutual suspicion.

'Industrial' development in villages is another potential flash-point between sectors of a community; the term itself is unhelpful and conjures images of dark satanic mills, rather than small-scale 'workshops'. Farming of course operates as a rural 'factory', with all the smells, noises and effluents attendant on large-scale industry. Farmers in particular can find themselves strangers within their own land: reviled for property dealing, misunderstood by a majority of neighbours with limited knowledge and interest in farming, and increasingly seen as recipients of dubious state subsidies like 'setaside', where they are effectively paid not to tend plots of land.

Racism is now recognized as a rural, and not just an inner-city, problem. Even BBC Radio 4's 'The Archers' has featured a campaign of intimidation against one of the characters, Usha Gupta, a solicitor of Asian origin who recently moved to Ambridge. "Hate mail and calls to the Archers studios, focused as they are on a fictional character in an imaginary village which for millions is the epitome of rural England, authenticate the storyline" (Kingston, 1995). Possibly this reaction arises from complex demographic changes: movement from the cities of people seeking escape from crime, which stereotypically may be pinned on a small number of black and ethnic minority perpetrators; the visibility of blacks within the 'white highlands', innate insularity of some rural communities and an extremist expression of NIMBYism. Fleeing to the country may be a conscious bid to escape from 'them'. Researcher Deborah Phillips observed that some estate agents around Bedford exhibited "strong indications of general racial bias – through refusal of access to details of properties", including 'higher status' houses in villages, to clients from a black or ethnic minority background. This was justified on the grounds that such people did not conform with their white and well-heeled stereotype of what a villager should be (Phillips & Karn, 1992).

Other social divides are more commonplace and perhaps not so dramatic. Parents and their dependants, especially teenage sons and daughters, can find rural living difficult. With few or no buses the car is critical for a social, work or sporting life. This can constrain parents who find themselves running a glorified taxi service, and aggravate young adults desperate to exert their independence.

The point is that rural communities, whether viewed in geographic or social terms, are complicated, dynamic and evolving entities. The development worker must therefore proceed with caution, always consolidating and reviewing progress in order to avoid misrepresentation of local feelings or over-reaching their certainty of popular backing.

Community Development and Certain Groups within Rural Society

Women constitute the traditional mainstay of volunteering in villages by running local clubs like the WI, Young Farmers, as well as community care schemes. But in the last years of the twentieth century women are under pressure, in financial terms having to seek paid work or, for personal reasons, aspiring beyond the home. The effect is the same because, as the Volunteer Centre (1991) claimed, 66 per cent of all volunteers in rural areas are women. In terms of rural community development, if fewer women have less time to dedicate to voluntary work then who will become tomorrow's volunteers?

Other difficulties for women in rural areas include low pay, virtually non-existent child-care provision, and insecure and seasonal work options. The implication for community development is that self-help may prove a more flexible avenue for increasing mutual support among women and even generating employment through such means as telecottages, home working or tourism associations that represent farmhouse bed and breakfast operators.

Physically and mentally disabled people face similar problems to those experiencing racism, in the sense that they are relatively few in number and scattered. In these circumstances there are high costs associated with specialist provision; and the range of individual problems experienced militates against individual solutions on grounds of cost or even the difficulties of recruiting staff to serve rural locations. For those suffering a physical disability there can be virtual incarceration in their homes, because the village hall, the pub or bus are not accessible to them. Mental handicap and mental illness can carry their own isolation on account of stigma, ignorance – 'is it catching' – and prejudice. Those experiencing mental illness also have to contend with centralized provision of counsellors and specialists: how can you afford to reach them and how do you manage the journey given abysmal public transport service. And if you are depressed or recovering from a 'breakdown' the last thing you are likely to want to face is a major expedition to seek treatment away from familiar territory. If hospitalization becomes necessary, usually within a town, then this represents a further alien environment with which to contend. The main implication for rural community development, therefore, is how it is possible and desirable to involve, empower and cater for those with special needs. Otherwise swathes of the rural population can be 'drowned out' by a vociferous minority.

Young adults can find village life hard to bear, often with no jobs, limited prospects, few affordable houses to rent or buy, and a restricted local social life. The village for many young people is a very public 'goldfish bowl', where non-conformity is glaringly obvious, conservatism the norm and where rumours about relationships can spread like wildfire. The school-village 'divorce' begins at an early age with pupils travelling away to their education; and by the time higher education might be considered, the divergence is complete. As young people increasingly look away from the village so local connections are weakened and eventually severed.

Problems for young adults in rural areas include homelessness, often as a result of family disputes, and a feeling of alienation in which there is a sense of fatalism and an inevitability that they cannot influence or even contribute to decision-making in their communities.

Homosexual men and lesbian women are particularly vulnerable within small settlements where there is likely to be no support network, often extreme hostility and prejudice, and a lack of positive role models for young people to follow.

Older people. A similar sense of impotence may confront older relatives or dependent in-laws, who have to contend with the ground rules set by their host families. As more people seek a house in the country, and retire early, so areas of vulnerability are opened up: the husband dies after only a few years in the country – and statistically it is usually the male that goes first – leaving his wife, who may well not drive, physically and psychologically isolated in a strange land. For senior citizens the problems can increase through difficulties with personal mobility plus advancing loneliness.

Professor Clare Wenger, University College, North Wales (cited in Kolek, 1993) has categorized older people into five distinct groupings according to their supportive network. At best 'locally integrated' pensioners have long-established connections and help from family, friends and neighbours. At the other extreme 'private restricted' individuals, according to Wenger, live a reclusive existence that reflects "a life-long pattern of low levels of social interaction and migration" (Kolek, 1993). There is no reason to believe that such support networks are exclusive to older members of (rural) society. 'New' mothers, single parents and those who are house-bound for various reasons, will also have a variety of resources to call upon, and therefore have differing needs and concerns (Derounian, 1993a). Once again the rural community is seen to comprise many, varied, overlapping and interactive component parts.

Theoretical Perspectives on the Composition of Rural Society
So far the discussion has ranged across various aspects of differentiation, potential and actual conflict or tension within villages. It is equally necessary to look at the spectrum of theoretical perspectives that underlie our understanding about the way in which society operates. In the same way that the 'rural community' does not exist, it can also be said that a 'true' picture of the functioning of such communities is impossible, because it will depend upon the starting point of the development worker or viewer. A mountain when seen from different angles, from above and below, presents different faces and impressions. Community workers will have their own perspectives on the nature of society, their

part in it and their assumptions before reaching decisions. Different standpoints will profoundly alter the reasons for intervention and means of taking action.

Table 1b   Models of Power in Society: A Summary

Pluralist	Power distributed between competing elites infused to varying degrees with meritocracy and forming checks upon each other. Democratically elected political elite predominates.
(Power) Elite	Rule by an elite dedicated to preservation of its own power and privileges. Democracy thereby reduced to a sham. The 'Establishment' (a British variant of this theory) exists, regardless of changes in government, as an unaccountable social elite drawn largely from the public schools and is always in power.
Ruling Class	The Marxist approach. Political control by a cohesive economic class (the owners of the means of production) which shares a common capitalist ideology.

Source: Coxall & Robins, 1994.

There are a number of theoretical approaches which underlie our perceptions of society. You may believe there is a relatively even distribution of power in the political arena and that decisions are made as a result of fair competition between interested stakeholders. Or you may take the view that any balance of power is compromised by the advantages of political or economic elites. Power is interpreted here as "the ability of one person or group (A) to get another person or group (B) to do as A wants" (Lawton & Rose, 1991): a central preoccupation for those working on behalf of rural communities!

The Democratic Ideal
If you agree with the pluralist view of the world you will contend that political power is widely, although not evenly, spread and that there is no monopoly on decision-making; the latter process involves competition and bargaining between different interests. In local government, for example "we might find groups composed of councillors, officers, local businessmen and women, client groups, voluntary agencies, all attempting to get their views accepted" (Lawton & Rose, 1991). There is a broad consensus regarding the objectives of the political system, and conflict is normally resolved via the ballot box, or through other peaceful means. Pluralists do concede, however, that a political elite, in the form of members of the Cabinet and senior civil servants, reigns supreme over business, financial and other interests. But it is critical to recognize that, according to

pluralists, the "governing elite acts within the powerful constraints of regular elections, and, between elections, of the countervailing influence of public opinion" (Coxall & Robins, 1994).

While pluralism provides only one interpretation of the way in which societies work (just one glimpse of the 'mountain') not even all pluralists hold common beliefs. Some of them view society as a bicycle which, although inherently unstable, can remain upright because of dynamic equilibrium between competing groups. On the other hand there are those who do recognize that groups and individuals may have differential access to contacts, information and people in positions of authority. Furthermore, argument exists as to whether the State is a neutral arbiter between competing groups or whether, in fact, it promotes its own interests.

Pluralists are criticized by 'non-believers' because they "unfairly distinguish between legitimate rule and illegitimate protest, and term 'extremist' those of whom they disapprove" (Ball, 1988). Think, for example, about contemporary criticism levelled at the suffragettes for their actions in pursuit of votes for women; the Greenham Common protests against nuclear weapons; or the poll-tax riots of the late 1980s; mass demonstrations against the export of live animals; Greenpeace sailing into dangerous waters on account of French nuclear testing in Polynesia. Hindsight may lend respect, credibility, and honour, but at the time many participants have been variously dubbed clowns, lunatics, nuisances, or even common criminals.

Rulers and Ruled

The elitist view is simple: there are the rulers and the ruled. "The smaller group, the political elite, controls the majority" by more or less legal means (Ball, 1988). An oligarchy, or small minority holds sway by virtue of its capability, ruthlessness, determination and commitment. The elite protects its own by reinforcing itself with recruits from within, or from a common social and cultural background. So the elitist model would point to the public school or Oxbridge background of leading political figures, civil service mandarins and senior figures in the military. A 1992 survey conducted by the *Economist* magazine confirmed that 66 per cent of people in top jobs across politics, the arts, business and finance had attended public schools, and 54 per cent were Oxford or Cambridge graduates.

In the rural context landowning is closely identified with political power; to a lesser extent farmers can be seen as part of an elite that controls land capable of development in and around villages. But there is some doubt over whether one elite dominates or whether a series of different elites rule in differing spheres.

Ball (1988) notes how "elitists differ from the pluralists on the crucial point of the concentration of power; they differ essentially from the Marxists over the sources of that elite power".

A variation on the elitist model was put forward by Ray Pahl (1970) who extended the Orwellian idea that all animals are equal but some are more equal than others. He suggested that there are 'gatekeepers' who open or shut doors in different spheres of life, thereby 'managing' approaches to power and decision-making. Such managers might include councillors and their paid officers – planners, surveyors, educationalists, etc. – civil servants and others with the keys to the doors of knowledge and policy determination. A planning officer, for example, will be aware of the procedures involved in gaining planning per-mission: statutory deadlines and criteria that must be adhered to; sub-committee and full planning committee consideration given to applications, or even dele-gated powers vested in some planning officers to determine certain types of development proposals. In this case a development control officer understands the system and its rules. According to Pahl (1970) "the controllers, be they plan-ners or social workers, architects or education officers, estate agents or property developers, representing the market or the plan, private enterprise or the state all impose their goals and values on the lower participants". . . within society.

Structuralism - the Marxist Viewpoint
Marxists subscribe to the theory that economic power determines political control. Economic and political power is seen to be within the grip of a small ruling class. Structuralists point to conflict within society as inevitable, between for example owners of the means of production in pursuit of profit and an exploited workforce. But the state will attempt to mitigate the worst effects of this division of political power, and to appease those who might otherwise attempt to disturb the *status quo*. Lord Vinson's quote about the Government's Rural Development Commission (see Chapter 4, page 55) is telling in this respect – that this quango exists to soften the cutting edge of the market in its effect on rural areas and not fundamentally to intervene. Remember too the charges (again in Chapter 4) that much rural development is small in scale, accepts the existing balance of power and, as structuralists would argue, it represents 'window dressing' rather than, as pluralists would have us believe, a genuine extension of democratic inclusion. So regeneration schemes, as an example, might be viewed by Marxist commentators as a social pressure-cooker lowering the temperature on troubled estates like Meadowell in Newcastle-upon-Tyne, but not funda-mentally changing circumstances. It would be seen as a sort of damage limitation exercise keeping the lid on a powder keg. Structuralists believe that society is in a dynamic state of continual conflict between master and servant, ruler and ruled,

the haves and have-nots. "To Marxists, elections are simply a ritual which confer neither real power nor even ultimate control on voters, merely the illusion of influence" (Coxall & Robins, 1994).

Corporatism
Corporatism puts forward the notion that the expertise of different groups of employers, unions, pressure groups, voluntary bodies, is utilized by the State in decision-making. The State gains from the expert knowledge and collaboration of these bodies and, in exchange, those organizations receive a foothold on the formulation and implementation of policy. So there is a symbiosis between state and outside interests. For Ball (1988) "corporatism implies that the state is not, as the Marxist claims, a repressive means of coercion but a means of engineering consent". For agencies involved in community development, corporatism offers the prospect of 'insider dealing', an ability to influence results in return for assistance and expertise to the state. The call by central government, in 1995, for interested countryside bodies to contribute their ideas to the rural white paper could therefore be construed as an exercise in corporatism (or indeed pluralism). An invitation to sit at the 'top table' also carries the threat that the offer can be withdrawn, if the 'guest' proves 'antisocial' or unbending. The National Trust, for example, now espouses an active campaigning role, but the paradox for the Trust is that "by becoming more openly involved in the political arena, it could jeopardise the unique access it has to the corridors of power" (Morrison, 1995).

Conclusion
This chapter introduces some of the complexities surrounding rural communities and shows how they can be differently constructed and perceived. The community development activist must be aware of these complications, and the nuances of working within small settlements. There also has to be self-recognition of what a development worker wants, and is capable of achieving. It is essential to confront and assimilate personal preferences and prejudices and always to seek to reflect broader local opinions and aspirations. Equally important is the realization that those you work with have their own views, prejudices and preconceptions, which must be understood and accounted for. Community worker know thyself, and seek to understand the world around you from the circumstances and evidence experienced; not the other way around by attempting to fit the facts into a pre-determined theory or mould. As Alan Ball (1988) concludes: the conflicting theories of power already discussed "have strong normative overtones; these theories are not merely concerned with what is but what should be. Given the ideological framework of the investigators, no approach to the study of political power is value free; political enquiry is not a neutral occupation". The same can be said of community development.

Chapter 2

Internal Agents and Structures

This chapter reviews village institutions in order to gain an understanding of who exerts power within a community. It also explains why community development activists need to be aware of, and probably court, such individuals and organizations if they are to succeed in encouraging local interests. It is essential for development workers to recognize the nature of the currents that they are stepping into. The following list of societies, clubs and organizations is not definitive of all the bodies to be found in every village. Included are the most ubiquitous and clearly relevant to rural community development, but each locality will require its own audit of key agents or 'players' in the vicinity. It is also important to recognize the 'hat phenomenon', whereby the same people turn up wearing different 'hats' so, for example, a school governor might also be a parish councillor and an active member of the Young Farmers Club.

> Michael and Hilary Winter live in the small west Devon village of Exbourne (population 300). Mike (aged 40) chairs the Parish Council and Playing Fields Committee; he is also a lay Reader for the Church of England, a preacher on the local Methodist circuit and steward at Exbourne chapel. Until recently he was a school governor. Hilary, meanwhile, is Secretary to the playgroup and Methodist church, and an active member of the WI and Parent Friends Association.

In a small place people have to double up, because there may be no-one else to turn to. This is why a development officer must tread carefully: persuade a few and you may well influence a greater number; alienate a minority and you could fall foul of many within the community. As an example of this, landowners and farmers may be few in number but they are likely to exert critical control over the availability of buildings and land, and land with development potential in particular; so they must be drawn into most ventures if they are to come to fruition.

The Parish and Town Councils

To all intents and purposes Parish and Town Councils operate in identical ways; the only difference is that larger parishes tend to be represented by a town council. While "some councils are run entirely on a voluntary basis with no paid staff and little expenditure, others represent communities of over 30000 people, may have a budget of more than £1 million and expenditure and staffing levels per head of population similar to the smaller district councils" (Derounian, 1993c). During 1995, for example, the Environment Minister sanctioned the creation of new parish councils in substantial settlements like Newbury, Exmouth, Billericay and Dover. There are around 8100 local councils in England with 70000 elected representatives. Parish and town councillors are democratically elected – or in 44 per cent of cases co-opted – to the third tier of local government, the parish councils. These local councils carry their own responsibilities and powers, in common with county, district and central government authorities. Since 1894 parish-level councils have existed in rural areas of England, and in some urban ones too. The Welsh 'equivalents' are the Community Councils, which unlike their English counterparts have no statutory responsibilities. A list of services provided by local councils in England is shown in Table 2.

Table 2   Services on which Councils Spent Money in 1989/90

Percentage of councils spending money on:

Churchyards/burial facilities	Lighting	
Signs and notice-boards	Dealing with litter	
Seats and shelters	War memorials	
Outdoor recreation	Information services	
Open spaces/greens/commons	Local newsletters	Community surveys
Village/community halls	Entering competitions	Allotments
	Maintaining footpaths	Roadside verges
47 – 56%	**28 – 33%**	**19 – 23%**

Source: Ellwood *et al.*, 1992

So far as rural development is concerned, the essential point is that parish councillors are accountable to their electorate through the ballot box. It has to be said though that the turnout for parish elections is very poor. Nevertheless councils are there to serve their constituents, not to plough their own furrows regardless of local opinion. Although that is an ideal position, in practice parish councils are popularly seen as parochial, ineffectual and small-minded. This is unfair given the fact that "three quarters of all local councils own land and/

---

or buildings, including one third of the smallest councils" (Ellwood *et al.*, 1992); and that these councils were estimated to have had in excess of £100 million at their disposal during 1990.

Some councils, however, pride themselves on not raising local taxation via the Council Tax. Yet there is a simple equation here: if a council fails to generate finance, then it will also fail its parish in not being able to assist the village hall, sports clubs, transport schemes or affordable housing developments. There has to be a line negotiated between profligacy and the absence of local funding.

Parish councils have specific legal powers, for example, in relation to the provision of cemeteries, notice boards, seating, outdoor recreation, village greens and community halls. As Table 2 shows, during 1989-90 roughly half of all parishes spent money on that range of facilities. In addition they can use discretionary powers, for example in committing money towards community-run projects of all types – environmental, community and cultural initiatives – including the restoration of redundant buildings to workspace. They also have a right to be consulted on all planning applications for their areas. As 'statutory consultees' they can submit comments on forward planning matters – Structure and Local Plans – plus individual planning applications.

A Councillor must be nominated by a number of electors and then receive enough votes in a 'first past the post' contest to gain a place on the council. Alternatively, in the absence of a full slate of candidates, constituents can be co-opted. The latter mechanism is attractive to parishes because it saves cash and also means that existing councillors can choose who they approach, rather than being at the mercy of the electorate! The poor turnout at parish elections again casts doubt on the representativeness of parish authorities: "it is estimated that as many as 45% of parish council seats are uncontested at elections and that 30% of councils are unable to fill the available seats" (Everitt, 1995). But it should also be said that the proportion of the electorate voting for parish councillors is on a par with those for district and county council contests, and better than the turnout for Euro-elections.

Traditionally councils have been seen as apolitical, when independent councillors act on behalf of electors; but increasingly local councils have become politicized. It is now not uncommon to find parishes reflecting the district and county council patterns of caucuses, pre-meeting meetings, ruling party committee chairs and proportional representation on working groups. Henry Gillett (1995), a labour town councillor from Skipton, sees another danger when "it is almost a confidence trick to stand for election to town or parish council as an independent candidate when, for example, one is chairperson of the local Conservative

Figure 2.1 The parish council: talking shop for local worthies?
(Cartoon by Simon Stern, courtesy of the Inkshed; first appeared in *Country Life*, 30 September 1995)

Association. Such unacceptable behaviour has, to my certain knowledge, occurred".

So 'parish pump politics' is not without its drawbacks. Councils tend to be seen as dogged by inertia, and slaves to conservatism with large or small 'C's and there are question marks about how representative their composition is (see the discussion in Chapter 1, concerning the possibility of elites, vested interests and self protection). Because councillors are unpaid and act out of civic duty or personal interest, these posts can attract those with time on their hands – the retired in particular – and militate against others with children or full-time jobs. That is how parishes come to be seen as guardians of the *status quo*.

The Clerk to the Council is in a pivotal position. Often the only paid (part time) employee of the parish council, a clerk must hold the council together by arranging meetings and sub committees, writing agendas and minutes, responding to requests for comment on a bewildering range of 'plans' for Community Care, waste disposal, transportation, policing and so on. A clerk must also ensure that a council is acting legally! So he or she performs the virtually impossible function of 'jack of all trades' – a sort of executive 'whipper in'. At the same time a clerk may have paid jobs to hold down as well as family responsibilities.

The Clerk to the small Parish of Elmdon and Wendon Lofts in Essex (population 400) noted recently that "with constant communications from the local District Council to deal with, such as planning applications and decisions which require action and distribution to council members who live seven miles away... in some cases, it is becoming almost like a full time job", and all for £700 annual salary (Jenner, 1995).

Many parish councils – and in the very smallest places, parish meetings, which convene only infrequently – are affiliated to the National Association of Local Councils (NALC). The latter operates through constituent county associations, like the Hampshire Association of Parish Councils, in a lobbying capacity, representing parish concerns to government at all levels. NALC itself is a member of another 'umbrella' campaigning group, Rural Voice (for more information see Chapter 3). The National Association has its own paid officers who advise on parish powers and responsibilities; at the local level county associations also have staff, often associated with Rural Community Councils (RCCs), who make the connections between outside agencies and parish councils.

The recent English Local Government Review points to an enhanced consultative role for the third tier of local government. The emphasis is very much on discussion and involvement, rather than ceding power: there should be regular meetings with the principal local authorities, improved consultation on highways and planning issues, the establishment of a clear consultative framework between local authorities and parish and town councils. Many primary authorities have been responding, for example, as in the case of Cumbria County Council in conjunction with Copeland Borough and the Cumbria Association of Local Councils, by creating charters of various kinds. They have established a Code of Practice "to provide a framework for co-operative and complementary action in the context of the County Council's commitment to the development of neighbourhood Forums and the Borough Council's commitment to devolved services" (Copeland Borough Council *et al.*, 1995). In addition, since 1991, the County has fostered the creation of 38 Neighbourhood Forums, "reflecting communities of interest". At the start forums were given two key tasks: "to act as the county council's consultative arm in getting public opinion on whatever issues the county council is involved in and to be a vehicle for getting local influence in the distribution of grants to the voluntary sector". Council department budgets "were brought together and then redistributed on a per capita basis to forum areas. Under a scheme of delegation which places the responsibility for decisions, via a sliding monetary scale on the neighbourhood unit manager, the neighbourhood services sub-committee or the county council's policy committee, forums are able to influence directly where money goes" (Burnet, 1995).

Money is an important inducement to attract the 'serious' politician or activist, and the Cumbria neighbourhoods initiative overcomes a central difficulty of parish councils – that by controlling the dispensation of financial 'peanuts', you get 'monkeys' to stand for office. But the Local Government Review points to increasing the **real** involvement of parishes in the operation of the other councils that influence life within individual settlements. This phenomenon of increased delegation is not unique to Britain: in Hungary for example, "although only a short while has passed since the foundation of local government, the passage of time has proved that it could manage its own fate more efficiently than the past centralized state administration and settlement policy" (Barakonyi, 1995).

For the would-be rural developer, the parish or town council **may** demonstrate many of the following strengths. It can crystallize and focus a sense of community; it is the form of government closest to the community; councils can, as the Cumbria example illustrates, act as a two-way communication channel between the parish and outside bodies and also sound out local opinions; the parish has direct connections with district, county or unitary councillors; there is also the possibility of providing some local services. In Taunton Deane District (South Somerset) as an example, many development control functions have been delegated, on an experimental basis to a number of parish councils.

Dunstable, Bedfordshire (population 35000), provides another longer-standing example of county council functions – relating to youth, museum and arts provision – that are devolved to the Town Council. To co-ordinate these services the Town retains a full-time paid Clerk and a range of other employees. Finally, parish councils can gain strength from meeting frequently (monthly), so that they can respond rapidly to significant issues. Research suggests that at least 1500 British rural communities have completed appraisals as a means of assessing local concerns and aspirations (Moseley, in press). Such evidence can provide parish councils with a mandate or strategic platform on which to act: informing comments about development proposals, grant assistance to projects, and partnerships with external agencies.

Love them or loathe them, parish councils cannot in most cases, be ignored by those seeking to work alongside local people. For example 75 per cent of parishes and town councils own land or buildings (Ellwood *et al.*, 1992). So they are likely to hold a central political and practical position in the formulation of proposals; and for many outside authorities the acid test of local commitment comes in the form of local council backing (money and/or support) for projects. A good community development worker can help transform the activities of a parish council and unlock its potential.

District, Unitary and County Councillors

These are representatives elected for the people by the people. They will serve a number of parishes and some thousands of constituents. In towns you will find several councillors covering the community. Each will represent a 'ward' or geographical area. Their primary purpose is to express local concerns to the relevant authority on which they sit. Councillors act as a two-way communication channel between a village and the external powers; they will attend parish council meetings to report on district or county business and to take back opinions on planning and other local council matters. Councillors are valuable allies in seeking grant aid and influence over strategic and immediate council actions. They can have access to local authority officers in ways that ordinary members of the public would almost certainly find impossible.

A major problem in contacting the right people in county, unitary and district authorities and getting them on your side is the simple fact that many people do not know who is responsible for what. Unfortunately the answer in reality is often less than clear. Broadly speaking shire county councils deliver social services, education, strategic planning, highways and economic development. A number of districts or boroughs then comprise a county area. These districts cover council housing, detailed planning matters, environmental health, sports and leisure provision and economic development. But immediately there are overlaps, in relation to tourism promotion, and exceptions for example when counties determine applications for mineral extraction and waste disposal sites. So the rural activist must gain a clear understanding of who does what in the local authorities in order to direct energies in a productive manner.

Councillors, as previously noted in relation to parishes, are political creatures with a large and small 'P'. Most will have a party affiliation and, thereby, varying degrees of influence. Your independent councillor might be a good constituency worker, but a lone voice on a district council. As such it is insufficient to gain their backing and you must ensure broader support, say, from the controlling party. What the local member can do is to attend various committees and the full council, at which matters of local relevance are being decided: closure of the school, housing association scheme, proposed tourist attraction in the community. However, political dogma can 'blow off course' statements from a councillor, so that they don't reflect local opinion. From the standpoint of the community or of community workers, the essential message is councillors are there to serve, and should be used to present concerns and aspirations to appropriate authorities.

The Village Hall Committee

A hall or community centre can perform an essential role in the public life and coherence of a community. It is a neutral meeting point – as opposed to a church hall – that offers the possibility for a range of activities: sports, meetings, pre-school play, lunch clubs for the elderly and even a location for services like the village shop. The control of a village hall is governed by its history. It may be run as a charity, with its own charity registration number, purposes and appointed trustees; the latter often reflect the users of the hall, in terms of WI representation, badminton club and so on. On the other hand a community centre might be in parish council ownership, the property of the Women's Institute, or of the church or chapel. Charitable status opens up the possibility of grant aid from other charities, like the Gulbenkian and Joseph Rowntree Foundations, and local authorities, whereas other types of ownership restrict the avenues for assistance. Also a 'trust deed' ensures open access by the community to the hall for community benefit; in contrast WI, parish council and other forms of control will inevitably favour their own particular uses and may oppose, or even prevent, some clients from gaining access.

In terms of rural development village halls offer the potential for multiple use. This is especially important given the decline in conventional rural services where, for example, "unless you counted the church there was no other community centre but the pub. The primary school had been axed and sold off for conversion" (Clarke, 1989). There are examples of day centres for older residents operating in halls, which allow interaction across the generations, perhaps drawing in children and grandchildren as volunteers. In this instance the location is the vehicle for community participation. Likewise there are community-run post offices and shops based in village halls. These services can benefit the most vulnerable members of rural society: the elderly, poor, and handicapped. Community plays and pantomimes raise other possibilities for building up community identity through enjoyment and use of a public building.

The major issue confronting hall committees is the tension that exists between breaking even and attracting custom. Do you adopt the 'Robin Hood' principle and exact differential pricing from customers: one fee for authorities (parish council) and branches of national bodies (WI, Young Farmers) and another for the play-group, lunch club? This policy brings problems when some groups become disgruntled at paying more, and there is also the danger of perceived or actual favouritism. Alternatively fixed pricing may militate against the smallest and most fragile clubs, which might simply not have the available finance. Another difficulty is in deciding what are allowable uses for the hall: the classic dilemma surrounds the staging of discos which are lucrative but 'dangerous', on account of possible vandalism, drunkenness, noise and other anti-social behaviour. Here is a social division within rural society potentially writ large.

The Women's Institute
The National Federation of Women's Institutes (NFWI) works via county federations comprising the individual WI branches. The NFWI is another founder member of Rural Voice. WIs exist to promote social support, education and training amongst women. Denman College in Oxfordshire is the Federation's residential base for a wide range of self-improvement and adult education courses, from cookery to assertiveness.

In recent years WIs have been keen to revise their 'jam and Jerusalem' image. While hymn-singing and home-cooking remain, some of the resolutions put to national conferences, for example, care in the community and domestic violence, have been highly topical and contentious. So whereas the National Federation is busy updating its image and activities, it is firmly based on the more traditional actions from its individual branches. Outside speakers are central to most WI meetings and lecture on women in business, environmental and planning issues, or topics related to domestic science. Of course not all WI-sponsored adult education and leisure pursuits are formalized or building-based. What a WI branch can foster is a network of friendships and contacts.

County federations produce regular newsletters which provide an excellent means of reaching members and, again, gaining snapshots of their needs. During the 1980s Devon RCC distributed a shopping survey in this way to branches and used the returns to compare village shop and supermarket prices, convenience and overall customer service. Potentially (and actually) WIs hold an important function in rural community development, for focusing and articulating the concerns of women. They also have the ability to draw women from across the age range and from diverse backgrounds.

Young Farmers' Club
In common with WIs the individual Young Farmers' Clubs (YFCs) tend to draw membership from several villages or parishes. As with the NALC and NFWI, the Young Farmers operate at three levels: a national one reinforced by county-based organizations, which in turn consist of scores of local branches. The National Federation is yet another participant body in Rural Voice but its main purpose is to promote the well-being of young people in rural areas. 'Young **Farmers**' is now something of a misnomer, and like agriculture itself, the organization has had to diversify. So YFCs seek to attract teenagers from across rural society and not solely from farming.

YFCs serve a social and educational purpose by arranging barn dances, quizzes, ploughing competitions, treasure hunts and also training in countryside pursuits and crafts. They also draw strength from ties with agricultural colleges. So the Young Farmers seek to move with the times while retaining links with their agricultural roots. Importantly YFCs are non-partisan in the sense that they are not aligned, as for example are the National Farmers' Union (NFU) or Country Landowners Association (CLA), with strict farming and land-owning interests. Some members however, may well farm in their own right or be related to farmers; their connections and interests, say, in the provision of affordable homes for young local adults, can make them ideal 'friends at court' in approaching those who might be critical to a scheme's success, like landowners.

The Young Farmers' Clubs may represent younger people's opinions in the same way that WIs can voice the needs of some women. So through the range of clubs that exist in villages, the rural developer is able to penetrate local society and painstakingly put together the pieces of the community jigsaw.

Sports Clubs
Sport can be a social leveller. The village soccer or cricket teams, badminton and rugby sides can all contribute to a sense of shared purpose and local identity. Sport provides a reasonably painless way for newcomers to gain a toe-hold in a community, and sporting activities enable people to engage in physical exertion as a precursor to social interaction. Of course this is an over-simplification and cliques can emerge amongst players, but the possibilities for community access should not be ignored.

Success at sport can also provide a valuable flag or emblem of wider regeneration. In this respect there can be a strong cultural dimension; think for example of Gaelic football in Ireland, Scottish curling and so on. Success in one sphere can engender a sense of pride, leading in turn to increased self-confidence and a belief that constructive change is possible. In addition clubs may own land and buildings potentially of use for other purposes (workspace, housing, play areas).

Yet clubs comprise far more than just the players. There are the committee people who make selections, organize training, social and fund-raising events, grounds' maintenance and ensure discipline. Supporters are the 'extended family' that turn out to see 'their' team, provide the cricket teas, seek sponsorship for new kit, and convey a sense of pride in its achievements to the wider world.

The Village School and Pre-School Playgroup
The connections between school and community are dealt with in detail as a case study (see Chapter 9), so the present section merely outlines this key internal

village institution and its component parts. Aside from emotive assertions that the primary school is the heart of the community, there is no doubt of its potential for promoting community development. Classrooms can house adult education sessions, or perhaps a shared information technology base (telecottage) as is the case at Crickhowell High School, Powys and Bellingham, Northumberland. Such initiatives not only foster self-help but also represent a meeting point between school and community; other ventures might include the staging of plays, sports events and various meetings of, say, the chess club, WI, or residents' association.

The school is a focus for a great deal of talent, shared concern and commitment. The Governors have legal responsibility for its overall activities and direction although, of course, their actions are prescribed by central government legislation. Governors are elected or appointed to serve distinct constituents: the parents, a council, a church, staff or Parent Teacher Association (PTA). The idea is to have an informed group capable of looking at the school and its needs in the round. The governors are 'gatekeepers' to the use of school property for community ventures.

A PTA complements the work of the governors and is strongly associated with fund-raising for new equipment, books, a play area and so on. It also seeks to raise money through social activities, like the school fête, quiz nights and discos. Such events draw people together with the ultimate aim of improving the school; they play on self-interest, in the sense that parents and former pupils are likely to be predisposed to help. The PTA may also lobby and contribute to school inspections in a way that governors cannot, because of their statutory responsibilities.

Parents can assist in curriculum coverage and development and thereby overcome some of the disadvantages of those very small schools where a handful of teachers are expected to be knowledgeable across the range of subjects. Skills like arts and craft work, local history, musical ability, and soccer training can all enrich the curriculum and involve parents by utilizing genuine talents. Teachers and ancillary helpers like nursery nurses, 'dinner ladies', and 'lollipop' attendants may well be parents, or otherwise from within the host community. So the school is a job creator and not just the passive recipient of charity.

Continuity is an important aspect of the role of a school in its community and also in relation to rural development in general. It is therefore important to forge real connections between first school and any pre-school playgroup that exists through visits to the school by toddlers and parents, for example to school plays, or by teaching staff going to the playgroup. Such exchanges should increase the likelihood of the school surviving and maintaining a lively and challenging education for pupils. A further potential link is with churches, and the Church of England (CofE) in particular. Many primary schools are still Church owned and part-funded, but beyond this connection there is the possibility of broadening pupils' experience so that their moral and spiritual welfare is not ignored.

Local Businesses

These are likely to be many and varied, including shops, farms, manufacturing, bed and breakfast and other tourist operations, a local pit, craft businesses, as well as self-employed builders, plumbers and accountants. In a rural context many companies will be small businesses with fewer than five employees. The discussion about sustainability (see also Chapter 6) necessitates networking on the part of village businesses in order to reinforce the local economy. This is a variation on the 'use it or lose it' slogan, that by utilizing services within an area – sub-post office, farm produce, language translation and so on – individual companies can generate and contain profits locally.

Companies are significant to individuals and an area, not least because of their job creation. This economic link can be capitalized on for rural development purposes. Local company employers are unlikely to be able to hide behind distant personnel officers, and can therefore be more readily approached for assistance. Their social consciences may also be 'pricked' in very personal ways at the cricket game, wife-to-wife, and so on. Contacts like these do, of course, require tact and discretion, and the downside of access is 'begging-bowl' fatigue – always being expected to contribute to every local cause. But potentially such social interaction can match the economic networking amongst local operators. In this respect help in kind from building work at cost, word-processing, or free legal advice, can be as valuable to community project and sponsor alike.

Multiple use is now a fact of rural business life, with the general store combined with, for example, a post office, garage, pub, tourist information point or tele-cottage. Multipurpose working offers a way forward for individual ventures, so they feed off each other's proximity. It is also attractive to potential customers as a 'one-stop-shop'; so that many enquiries can be dealt with at one location. Finally, as with the WI and Young Farmers' movements, the private sector has its own national body, Business in the Community (BiC), which is able to draw on the considerable clout of managing directors in companies like Bass, BNFL, ICI, Blue Circle and Lloyds Bank. As the name implies BiC encourages businesses to put back into the communities from which they draw their success. Given the movement of people back into the countryside, and the consequent desertion of the cities, many top managers and other potential contributors now live in villages and commute to work. Their presence opens up new possibilities for seeking private-sector support for rural development.

Commuters, commonly disparaged as parasites on their host community, can also help by sharing transport with those who are carless; an example would be the Gower Voluntary Transport scheme in south Wales. Regular town and city travellers could also assist in the bulk buying of goods from a 'cash and carry', in order to stock a community-run shop. Rural developers must always look to the possibilities and not be automatically seduced into over-simple stereotypical prejudgements that commuters or holiday home owners are necessarily 'bad'. In the Welsh example of English-owned second homes being fire-bombed, has the arson been misdirected? Would local families really want to live in those properties that were dilapidated and isolated from all human contact and services?

Churches, including the Parochial Church Council
The Parochial Church Council (PCC) is not to be confused with the parish council as it is exclusively concerned with the running of the parish church and has jurisdiction over any land holdings or associated buildings. A PCC can nevertheless still play an important part in rural development, for example, by making available land at below market value for the construction of affordable houses.

Church Council connections with the local Church of England (CofE) Diocese (or Bishopric), for example those based on Exeter and York, can also prove valuable in reaching the church hierarchy, grant aid (CROP funding) and, again, possible land and buildings like a redundant church-assisted school for community use. Since the publication of *Faith in the Countryside* (1990) the CofE and constituent dioceses have been sensitized to the needs of rural communities and reminded of their responsibilities to them. So in community development terms the Church, in principle, has an open door to be entered for assistance. The Archbishop of Canterbury has also created the position of Adviser on Rural Affairs, as an indication of his serious intent to tackle rural problems. The adviser edits a magazine, *Country Way*, which is well worth a look at for examples of good practice and of churches' direct action on rural inequalities. The clergy themselves constitute an important resource around which initiatives may coalesce. At Uffculme in Devon, for example, the Reverend Geoffrey Fraser gave initial momentum, during the 1980s, to the redevelopment of a working mill museum, which is now a substantial tourist attraction. Although vicars increasingly cover a number of parishes, they can still represent the last connection with officialdom and the outside world – after the school has gone, the bus service withdrawn, post office and shop boarded up.

As already noted in the village school section above, the church-school link can be of value to pupils, congregation and parents alike. Although this discussion has centred on the Church of England, this is not to deny the potential of non-conformist churches, and indeed of other faiths in contributing to self-help ventures. Geography and culture will influence the relative importance of different churches in differing locations and the would-be developer must recognize this fact and direct attention accordingly. In Ireland, for example, it is the Catholic church that has been closely aligned with co-operative and other rural development.

Civic and Amenity Societies and Residents' Associations

In larger communities especially there could well be a civic society acting as a local environmental watchdog. Such groups seek to influence strategic statements in Structure and Local Plans and will promote good architectural practice. They tend to be concerned primarily with conservation. The best societies are beginning to involve villages in wider environmental debates, for example in relation to Local Agenda 21 and sustainability (see Chapter 8 for more information on this topic). Societies can also exert a kind of constructive NIMBYism, by keeping a wary eye on planning standards and environmental quality; at worst they can represent the short-sighted views of the anti-development brigade, regardless of need for developments or sensitivity to design. In terms of rural development though, it may well be better to bring a civic society on side than to ignore it and potentially face brickbats as a result. Parish conservation groups as well as larger-scale organizations, like the British Trust for Conservation Volunteers, can also take positive and practical action to benefit a locality.

Youth Club

A youth club provides a different opportunity (from the Young Farmers) to engage young adults *en masse*, and to hear their ideas for community improvements. Youth clubs tend to cater for those in their early teens (12-15 year olds). Young people can, as discussed in the first chapter, feel alienated within their own villages because of pressure to conform in the very public 'goldfish bowl' of living in a small place, and because parish councils and other arbiters of power within the community tend to ignore the needs of the coming generation.

Teenagers, if registered at all, are likely to be seen as a nuisance. A youth club, which may often be connected to a church, can constitute a productive outlet for youthful energies and also harness the considerable talents and idealism of this age group, for example, in relation to local environmental action.

Local Charitable Trusts

Literally thousands of villages have their own charitable trusts. These result from bequests made in wills, often hundreds of years ago. At Chagford on Dartmoor, for example, there is Bunnamy's Bread Charity, originally established to ensure that the poor of the parish received an adequate supply of bread. Charitable trusts therefore operate under specific purposes and must do so if they are to retain charitable status. They are regulated by the Charity Commission. Trusts offer potential funding to initiatives of community benefit; some are international concerns, dispensing thousands or even millions of pounds like Leverhulme and Gulbenkian. Others are much more parochial and distribute correspondingly smaller sums. But the skill remains the same: to establish what a particular charitable trust is concerned with, what sums it can allocate and how often it meets to decide on grant offers. You should also find out who the trustees are, because personal contact is more likely to prove fruitful than sending a hopeful letter into the void. County Rural Community Councils and the London-based Directory for Social Change publish regular updates on individual trusts and how to approach them. But you must tailor your request, in terms of amount and type of project, to specific, likely trusts. Directed advances will prove more effective than a 'blunderbuss' approach.

Conclusion

Chapter 2 does not pretend to give some definitive listing of power-brokers existing in every village, nor has it attempted to give weight to the various players, because this will vary according to local circumstances. It has tried to convey the range and variety of local organizations and of their potential for aiding rural community development. A rich diversity of community groups and activities exists across rural areas.

A survey of 3000 'Village Halls in England' for example documented 65 different social, recreational, educational, sporting or general uses! These ranged from chiropody and blood doning sessions to bell ringing and drama classes, jumble sales, badminton and wedding receptions. On average sixteen activities take place in each hall. "Bearing in mind that 40% of the villages served populations below 600, this is testimony to the community spirit for which villages are noted." (ACRE, 1988)

The process of community development is a continual attempt to match up the pieces of a complex jigsaw so that a clear and comprehensive picture results. Only by 'beating the bounds' of who is there as a prospective helper, can you effectively turn rural development theory into practice.

Chapter 3

External Agents
and Structures

As traffic speeds along the A68 on its way to Scotland, it passes by the small border village of Otterburn (population under 1000). Otterburn nestles just outside the Northumberland National Park boundary and is perhaps best known as the site of a bloody confrontation between the English and Scots in 1388.

During 1992 I was the Rural Development Programme (RDP) Officer with a roving brief to encourage social and economic initiatives throughout the massive Rural Development Area (RDA) designated by government in 1984 as a means of directing assistance to locations suffering multiple disadvantage (for more on RDPs see Chapter 10). The post was part-funded by four districts and a county council and one of the sites eligible for Rural Development Commission funding, via the RDP, was Otterburn. I had become aware of Otterburn Mill, having already been involved in fund-raising for a local sports centre and also because we lived in a nearby community. Introduction to the mill was more by luck than judgement – an important ingredient to rural community action.

A number of things became apparent over a short period of time: the mill manager at that time, John Waddell, had tremendous enthusiasm for, and knowledge about, textile milling in general, and the history of Otterburn Mill in particular. In conversation he was able to bring the place alive; he had for example been born on site and over his lifetime had seen the decline of the business. By 1990 the internationally recognized woollens label of 'Otterburn Mill' was a name only as no weaving had taken place at the mill for some time. A shop retailed Otterburn material, made to original patterns, but all the machinery, including teasel carding machines, water wheel and tenter frames, were quietly rotting. Apart from buying woollen souvenirs, scarves, jumpers, etc., there was no other reason for visitors to stop at the mill.

Having toured the buildings with John Waddell I became convinced of the possibilities for a revival project. Apart from the significant numbers of tourists

---

driving past the 'front door', and its proximity to the National Park, there was also the magnificent collection of industrial archaeological artefacts; and in marketing terms there was the established 'Otterburn' name and the possibility of Ministry of Defence assistance on the back of their commitment to the local training area. So what was the next step?

In order to get the ball rolling I wrote direct to the National Trust (NT) Regional Director, with whom I had dealt amicably before, to gauge whether there might be any interest from his organization. The Director replied and left open a tiny 'window' of opportunity, that the Trust could only really consider involvement if persuaded of the 'historical value' of the site. To demonstrate this and to give a real flavour of the place, a site visit was arranged. The regional manager and his historic buildings adviser were accompanied by John Waddell. The two of them left enthusiastic about the possibilities, but they were met with extreme scepticism by their colleagues.

The project was not seen as being commercially viable, since there was no 'dowry' to go with the mill into Trust ownership, and some twenty family shareholders actually wanted a return on their stakes in the business. Interest from the NT withered, so an alternative pathway had to be found. Too much rural development depends on the fragile enthusiasm of few activists, so efforts were made to broaden 'ownership' of the project.

A small, highly motivated, team of influential individuals, the Otterburn Mill Group (OMG) was organized with a commitment and focus on the task in hand. A Training and Enterprise Council (TEC) Director, who was also an Otterburn hotelier, displayed enlightened self-interest in joining a venture that could generate a major tourist attraction; and he was also able to tap into TEC funding. Next was the Tynedale District Council Tourism Development Officer, who had the brief to initiate new tourist enterprises and could provide a way into local authority advice on planning and other issues, as well as potential grant aid.   Third was an internationally recognized industrial archaeologist and developer of the ambitious Beamish Open-air Museum near Stanley, County Durham, who brought financial realism and expertise in the retention and conversion of historically sensitive properties. Next was the NT regional historic buildings officer, who maintained a personal interest in the site, whilst giving the group a foot in his organization's door. The Northeast Museum's Service Director joined and provided contacts and expertise related to the establishment of a working museum. John Waddell represented the owners, and obviously nothing could or should take place without their consent, knowledge and participation although the shareholders' attitude remained one of benign indifference. The final member was the Northumberland National Park archaeologist, who represented a source of specialist information and a channel into Park funding and wider County involvement (because the National Park was administered by a committee of Northumberland County Council). The RDP officer convened meetings and acted as Chairman and Secretary; he was also able to access RDC finance. Thus each member of the group was there willingly and for specific reasons, rather than being foisted on it as a representative of the agency in question.

The first substantive action of the OMG was to determine a brief for consultants, in order to commission a feasibility study. Such studies can get a bad press, telling people the obvious at great expense, and delivered by consultants interested in short-term financial gain rather than any commitment or responsibility for their findings. In this case, however, the group saw a feasibility study as a prerequisite to understanding how best to restore this historic property via a commercially viable business proposition. It was also recognized that such a study could prove invaluable, in terms of credibility, for subsequent approaches to interested (funding) parties. For grant-aid bodies themselves there was the advantage that they were being asked for relatively small sums (in the low thousands); they were seen to be supportive, while at the same time the commitment was limited to a study alone, without further automatic agreement to financing the implementation of findings. It constituted a mutually agreeable halfway house.

Representation of various agencies on the group smoothed the way for grant awards from the TEC, which was interested in possible job creation arising from a new mill museum. Tynedale Council also chipped in towards the study costs under its tourism and economic development budgets. Otterburn Mill Limited contributed on the basis of self-interest and potential diversification of the business. Finally, the Rural Development Commission supported the possibility of economic development in a remote location. This funding jigsaw, totalling around £15000 was pieced together on the basis that different bodies were supporting the same study in expectation of differing returns.

The feasibility study was completed during 1993 and, shortly before publication, the Rural Development Officer left to take up a new job. Would the report gather dust? Who would champion and drive forward the findings? In the event Tynedale Council, through its Tourism Officer, picked up the baton. And in 1995 she wrote explaining that the mill had been sold to an entrepreneur with "experience in the mill and retail business. He has big plans for the mill including retail, catering, heritage and a visitor centre/Tourist Information Centre. We got there in the end!" (Turner, *pers. comm.*). No doubt the saga is not yet over, but what are the lessons from this case study?

Specific Lessons from the Otterburn Project

First, rural development takes time; in this case spanning a period of five years. Second, persistence pays off. You have to think laterally, moving crab-wise at times, looking to probe the defences for an opening.

Widening ownership and commitment increases the capability of project initiators, and provides a more solid foundation rather than dependence on one or a few activists. While an individual can't be an expert in all aspects of a scheme, a team can cover the ground.

The Otterburn case also highlights the importance of enlightened self-interest to community development: a flat property market, restrictive planning controls and 'arms length' interest in the future of the company, encouraged collaboration over the future of the mill, in expectation of a sale of the property for financial gain to a developer – which has proved to be the case.

Help from External Agencies

Every village has its own key 'players' and activists but organizations outside a settlement can have considerable influence on what happens within a community. External agencies will exert differing potential impacts and it is important to gain a broad understanding of their purposes rather than becoming bogged down in the minutiae of individual operations. An agency's remit determines its actions: for example English Heritage (EH), a quango, exists to conserve England's heritage, and to encourage public enjoyment and understanding of historic artefacts. So detailed EH activities and expenditure must accord with these overall objectives. It is the same for registered charities such as Greenpeace, the RSPCA, Salvation Army, Barnardo's, in the sense that they must act within their stated charitable purposes, as sanctioned by the government 'watchdog', the Charity Commission. By stepping beyond its remit a body could be liable to legal redress or a rap over the knuckles by an Ombudsman, whose job it is to investigate maladministration.

The next, and highly visible, aspect of an organization is its ability to fund projects and programmes through grant aid or loans. In many ways this is the 'acid test' for agencies and whether they are worth approaching, and have money to offer. Community development activists have to be particularly careful not to lose the integrity, sense and 'shape' of their original proposals, in a headlong rush to secure financial help at all costs. It is all too easy to be seduced into stuffing the idea through a grant-aid 'sausage machine' that produces finance which will result in a scheme that bears little resemblance to the original idea. Another contemporary funding dilemma is the fact that more and more agencies are offering less and less. Many have become a source of assistance only in the last resort. Local initiative can so often be stifled at birth. That is why forms of assistance other than money can be so useful: sound guidance must complement finance even if the latter is available, otherwise scarce resources can be squandered in nothing more than a show of assistance (Chapter 8, on the Rural Action experiment, reinforces the importance of this point). Equally the Rural Development Commission offers grant and loan funding backed up by specialist business advice on the restoration of redundant buildings, for example, technical know-how related to thatching and other crafts, or how to improve the viability of a village shop and so on.

Practical help 'in kind' can prove invaluable: private sector provision of (specialist) equipment, land or buildings for potential development, or a county education authority offering 'moth-balled' school buildings for a community venture. Help-in-kind is a relatively straightforward way in which to tap local businesses, without the bureaucracy and delay of seeking cash via committees and senior management. Company executives, as noted in the previous chapter, live in country communities, although they may commute to town to work. Both direct approaches or, especially, indirect ones via children or partners can reap rewards.

Agency support for an initiative can lend credibility and exert leverage on other agencies. A potential funder is likely to feel reassured if others have already committed themselves to a scheme, which goes back to the previous point about who will be first to throw their hat into the ring. Parish council funding can and should usually constitute the first piece in the funding jigsaw, for without a local expression of support, why should more distant potential helpers offer assistance?

Then there is what could be termed 'statutory smoothing': the award of planning permission, licensing and approvals of various kinds. These technicalities are essential if grants and help-in-kind are to turn an idea into reality. So an approach, to a local authority, for example, can 'kill several birds with one stone'. Grant aid could be sought from, say, an economic development budget, while specialist staff – tourism, conservation and development control officers – advise on particular aspects of a venture. Local government backing would also encourage others to follow suit.

The Nature of the Beast
Many agencies have a local presence but, as noted in Chapter 2, also operate under the national umbrella of a lobbying organization such as the Local

Government Association, the voluntary sector Rural Voice or private sector Business in the Community. It is not always easy for the rural community development worker to know which part of a large organization like a district council to approach in order to shift the levers of power in support of a local scheme.

Local Authorities

These are complex organizations, responsible for a wide range of services. They have legal and technical responsibilities, such as determining planning permissions, monitoring environmental health, waste collection and disposal, but these apparently defined duties are carried out within a highly politicized arena. Throughout the 1990s a charged atmosphere has engulfed the central and local government relationship. Conservative government policy reined in local expenditure and set spending assessments for local authorities which can only be breached on pain of financial ruin. The Government has enforced competitive tendering for services like refuse collection and road maintenance; with the result that, in the case of Berkshire County Council planning department, these duties are contracted out to a private consultancy. The whole system was thrown into the melting pot of local government review. *Status quo* is maintained in some of the English shires, but "from 1996 the majority of Great Britain will be served by district-based . . . unitary authorities" (Clark, 1995c). Therefore the dealings between central and local governance have been strained.

Tension is reflected within local authorities as well, both in the relationship between paid officers and elected politicians ('members') and in the political caucuses that differentiate councillors wearing distinctive political labels. As far as those engaged in community development are concerned, it is vital to identify 'where people are coming from'.

The theory is that paid officers advise elected politicians, who control policy and decision-making and execute these decisions. In reality, of course, nothing is in 'black and white', but merely shades of grey. In some instances officers exercise delegated powers, for example determining small-scale or non-contentious planning applications, without recourse to the politicians. Given the complexities of local government finance and legislation, the balance of power can easily shift, or be seen to revert, to technocrats. So those seeking to exert influence must be efficient in recognizing who to influence and when. Chief officers (Planning Officer, Treasurer, Chief Executive and so on) will, for example, meet regularly to decide on how to react to political preferences, whilst also setting their own agendas for consideration by councillors. At the same time a ruling party will have its own parallel caucus meetings at which committee chairs agree policy and voting tactics. Opposition parties and independent councillors will, no doubt, meet separately and *en bloc* to decide their own intentions.

Both officer and member deliberations – plus any public comment, lobbying, protest – will then feed into a series of sub and main committee discussions and decisions, leading up to ratification by the full council that comprises all of an authority's elected representatives. So a decision by councillors to save £1 million in a given year will be translated by chief officers into specific options, say, for a county council to close fire stations, reduce the provision of specialist teachers or contract out the promotion of tourism. The controlling group on that council would then reduce these suggestions to a sharper focus, perhaps concentrating on the closure of a substantial number of small schools, as happened in Warwickshire during 1995. These specific suggestions are then debated through various committees until the full council takes its definitive stance. The final decision then returns to the officers for implementation. So concerned individuals have a series of 'bites at the cherry', and one success in committee does not guarantee final 'victory' at full council.

At Stow-on-the Wold, Gloucestershire, Tesco put in a planning application for a supermarket during the late 1990s. There were strong lobbies both in favour (from local people) and against (town traders). District council planning committees refused the application, but the full council voted to grant permission. When the full council meets things can always change!

Pressure and lobbying must be directed, focused and sustained to ensure maximum potential success.

Departments within authorities, and indeed inside central government (see the National Park and MoD discussion in Chapter 4), do not necessarily 'sing from the same hymn sheet'; and neither do politicians with the same political affiliation. A planning officer concerned for the overall impact of a development, as an example, may differ in attitude towards a scheme from his tourism development counterpart; and both may run up against different (financial) arguments advanced by the treasurer.

Who are your natural allies and what power do they wield in the hierarchy? It is essential for a community development officer to foster contacts in local authorities and to keep these channels open and up to date. Organizations may seem anonymous but of course they are just a collection of individuals, each with their own personality, opinions and agenda. There will, almost certainly, be helpful and amenable individuals worth cultivating. It is easier to ask questions of someone you already know rather than making an approach to a stranger in relation to a delicate matter or a crisis. In Ireland, as an example, it is interesting to note in relation to planning that it is county councillors who discuss the content of a strategic Development Plan, which prescribes exactly where development can and cannot take place. Individual decisions on planning permissions then become a technical judgement made by the officers alone, but set entirely within the parameters of the strategic policies. So officers and members will prove helpful at different times.

This highlights a further important point, that early influence will succeed where late exertion cannot: outline planning permission concedes the principle of developing a particular site; full permission then fills in the detail. Likewise a National Park Plan will set down villages for development and restraint; once agreed these heavily influence subsequent individual development control decisions. So it is important to think strategically and influence early.

Quangos

There are peculiar public sector bodies, commonly called 'quangos' (QUasi-Autonomous Non-Governmental Organizations), or as one of them would prefer, a QUalified and Notably Gifted Operation (English Heritage, 1994). These are distinct from local and central government in the sense that they receive an annual budget from Parliament to carry out their remit – £99 million for English Heritage in 1994 – and are also controlled by political appointees, not elected representatives. English Heritage has fourteen 'Commissioners'; the Rural Development Commission eleven, with interests in the English countryside, including a Shropshire County Councillor, rural sociologist and the Chairman of Pennine Heritage. Commissioners, in common with a proportion of National Park representatives, are appointed by the Secretary of State for the Environment, according to their knowledge and expertise in a specific field. Nonetheless there still remains the whiff of central government 'placement' of political allies.

One of the major criticisms levelled at quangos is that they are anti-democratic, because they siphon power from elected representatives, answerable via the ballot box, to non-elected appointees. Why, for example, has it been necessary to create Urban Development Corporations to undertake inner-city renewal, or to finance housing associations, rather than giving local government the where-withal? Efficiency and cutting the Gordian knot of bureaucracy, is the answer from the central state; emasculating potential rivals is the counter claim from local authorities. Another accusation concerns the "enormous costly industry flourish-ing in . . . quangos full of people with dubious qualifications and grandiose job titles, who are determined to tell us what to do in the countryside and ensure that we do it!" (Fulford, 1995). It is at this contentious interface that the 'third sector' makes its appearance.

The Voluntary Sector

The voluntary sector acts as a vast and growing bridge between individuals and the state. As we have seen, local government functions are being hived off into the private and voluntary sectors. In relation to community care and homelessness, for example, many different charities are engaged in providing for people in need. So voluntary activity is politicized in the sense that the line between state action and responsibility on the one hand, and voluntary sector action on the other is constantly shifting. There is also the fact that "Government now provides one-third of the funding for the voluntary sector, and its power has been further enhanced by the National Lottery. Inevitably, such dependence has its price and many fear that missions to change society are being compromised by the need to keep government happy" (Mulgan, 1995). Charities are caught in a classic dilemma, that if the public sector withdraws services, is lobbying alone a correct and adequate response, or should voluntary bodies intervene in a practical sense to mitigate the worst effects, or even seek to substitute for state provision?

Of course voluntary bodies, or Non-Governmental Organizations (NGOs), vary enormously in size, scope, resources and political effectiveness. There have been specific charges that "tax privileges go not just to Save the Children but also to Eton, not just to the RSPCA but also to Covent Garden Opera House. In other words, privileges are given to services for the rich as much as to services for the poor" (Mulgan, 1995).

Equally, an agency like the Council for the Protection of Rural England (CPRE) is well known and thought to be influential in government circles. As the name implies, the focus for concern is on protection, preservation and conservation; urban renewal for example is seen as a means of reducing the pressure for development on greenfield and Green Belt sites. The CPRE is highly vocal and operates via county branches, but its voice is disproportionate to its membership, which stands at just 46 000.

On the other hand, there are the Royal Society for the Protection of Birds (RSPB) and National Trust (NT), in particular, that are substantial landowners, financially powerful and which boast an impressive number of members. The NT currently has in excess of 2.5 million paying members supporting the retention and maintenance of historic properties and landscapes. And of course a number of charities, like Oxfam, Help the Aged and Amnesty International, operate on the World stage. So voluntary neither equates with amateurism nor does it necessarily imply some 'tin-pot' agency living from hand-to-mouth.

One salutary story of inter-sector jockeying, comes from the 1980s, when Tom King was Environment Minister. He came to present awards to volunteer-run projects that had entered a national Village Ventures competition. The Minister was so impressed by the degree and variety of self-help evidenced by these projects that he was able to declare that no further public expenditure was needed in the English countryside! In this light it should be "recognised that the voluntary approach to rural community development is but one means to an end and one which inevitably has its limitations. It is predominantly consensual rather than conflictual in its approach and has a long-standing tendency to accept existing structures within society rather than oppose them" (Rogers, 1987). This highlights the continual tension between challenging the world as it is, and working towards change while at the same time acknowledging that present woes demand compromises to ensure that the most vulnerable are not totally lost and forgotten. Humanitarian aid to former Yugoslavia provides a good example – aid agencies have worked with local warlords to reach refugees in desperate need. They have had no choice but to compromise over the 'bigger picture', in the short term, in order to secure smaller-scale gains.

Voluntary agencies comprise an essential component of rural action: English RCCs and Councils of Voluntary Service (CVSs) are particularly relevant and active in promoting rural community development. These are charitable bodies operating in every shire county of England and delivering advice to parish councils, on village hall matters, self-help projects and the maintenance or restoration of village services. So RCCs can offer specialist advice on the intricacies of charitable registration, small grants for newsletter production, towards volunteer-run projects like 'community shops', environmental action and so on, or help with campaigning to retain a local school, post office, etc; and explain the powers and responsibilities of parish councils and village hall committees. Additionally they practise 'patchwork', through the employment of community development officers, and use and foster many of the 'tools of the trade' cited in Chapter 5.

The Private Sector

This is another sweeping heading that covers a multiplicity of companies, or businesses, both large and small. As far as community development is concerned private businesses are likely to fund or offer help-in-kind where they see a definite advantage, particularly in terms of good publicity or product promotion. At the very largest scale, companies want to be associated with success or a 'good cause', whether it is a premier division football team sponsored by a brewery like Scottish and Newcastle, or Calor Gas promoting Village Ventures competitions, which reward and publicize self-help projects, through Rural Community Councils.

As mentioned in the preceding chapter, the private sector in this country also combines under the banner of Business in the Community (BiC) to demonstrate input to and not just extraction from the locality. BiC uses high-level connections with 'the establishment', especially in the form of their President Prince Charles and the Duke of Westminster (who chaired a working party into the 'problems of rural areas', 1992, for BiC).

At a village or local scale, companies can be persuaded to offer help, based on their connections with the place, the fact that employees are likely to come from the particular community and, again, because the business wants to be seen to be acting generously and in support of local concerns; this might include advertising in the newsletter or help-in-kind for the village hall.

Having ranged across the sectors it may be useful to recap by using the exercise in Appendix I. It's called 'Take your Partners' and the idea is to look at the following three potential projects and decide, from the listing of external agencies, which organizations will be able to help each scheme and why. Each of the initiatives will have a roughly similar number of assistants, although some bodies might well appear in some or all of the lists. There is no 'right' answer but try to reason through your nominations.

General Lessons for Seeking Assistance from Outside Bodies
Any request for money or resources for a project must be tailored to specific agency purposes, remit, and priorities. In short you have to 'speak the same language' as the organization concerned. So it is useless to stress environmental benefits to an agency (like a TEC) that is primarily concerned with training and job creation.

Part-funding is a reality for most community development initiatives – often with no more than 20 per cent contributed by any one body – and necessitating the piecing together of a financial patchwork of assistance. In the case of the Otterburn feasibility study four agencies contributed to the overall cost.

Then there is the issue of capital versus revenue finance. Organizations tend to favour support for tangible, discrete, projects, such as the building of a village hall, or a swimming pool. What they invariably shy away from is revenue funding – paying for staff over an extended period or contributing towards running costs. To use an analogy, organizations will 'plant a tree' but rarely do those external funders 'water it'. This is an understandable but short-sighted policy, because once the hardware is in place (like a swimming pool) the really tough work begins in making it pay its way. And just how realistic is it to expect a community project to break even in the short-term? I am not advocating open-ended, but rather extended, short-to-medium term, subsidy to ensure that the investment in a sapling eventually bears fruit. Specialist advice can, of course, be just as valuable as money, for example free legal help from a solicitor or at-cost construction from a local builder. External bodies can therefore provide an essential complement to the internal dynamism and talents of local people.

A key task for the community development worker is to assist local people to develop the confidence and skills to deal with external agencies. This is sometimes termed capacity building. The Otterburn case study in particular highlights the point that organizations are made up of individuals. Contact with the National Trust itself didn't prove fruitful, but it did allow access to a helpful and committed individual. If you don't identify the right person first time, try another!

Chapter 4

Key Themes of Rural Community Development

In a progressive country change is constant. The question is not whether you resist change, which is inevitable, but whether the change should be carried out in deference to the manners, the customs, the laws, the traditions of people. (Benjamin Disraeli)

It is important to keep in mind the overall aim of this book: to help people appreciate, in a practical sense, what they can achieve, and to offer staff from external agencies techniques for working effectively alongside local communities. "Community development is about 'getting things done'... but it is also about the creative development of people – people working together to support each other, involving and giving power and responsibility to disadvantaged people, growing in confidence and competence through active participation, confronting inequalities in society" (Francis & Henderson, 1992). So rural community development is both a process, bringing about the "creative development of people" individually and collectively, and also generates a product – which might require "building a children's play area, saving a school, caring for people with a disability" (Francis & Henderson, 1992). This chapter will discuss key aspects of community development: top-down versus bottom-up ways of working, integrated activity, networking, ownership, sustainability and innovation.

Top-Down versus Bottom-Up

Top-down decision-making works on the basis that outside agencies know best and act accordingly. Michael Dower, a vice-president of ECOVAST, the European Council for the Village and Small Town, in 1991 condemned the impact of EU policies because "these programmes tend to be conceived in principle in Brussels; applied (within the constraint of those principles) by decision-makers in national capitals; and expressed at regional level, for regions which may contain a wide area and great variety of rural communities ... Many such regional programmes are distorted, and made to a greater or lesser degree irrelevant or even damaging to the needs of rural communities and the rural environment ..." He went on to cite the destruction caused by European (so-called) Integrated Mediterranean Programmes (IMPs); on Crete, for example, olive trees contributing to the 'traditional landscape' were ripped out to make way for avocado plantations, never before seen on the island. "The avocado project has collapsed amid the laughter of the local people" (Dower, 1991). Dower extended this message by contending that "local people often have a far better feel for what is appropriate and sustainable in their area than do governments" (Dower, 1995).

There is also the critical importance of participation as opposed to passive consultation (Hawtin *et al.*, 1994). As the respected community development practitioners David Francis and Paul Henderson make crystal clear: "To be effective, 'community involvement' must not be some peripheral process, serving to legitimise a predetermined programme or to add a little icing to the cake. Rural development must have at its core the active development of people and communities for them to take on the role of planners, decision-makers and key actors and, ultimately, to be the prime beneficiaries" (1992). In this regard it is encouraging to see the Government's Rural Development Commission pressing for community involvement to extend "beyond formal consultation exercises for local plans and individual planning applications to a more active participation in the planning process" (Teasdale, 1995). And in Northern Ireland the Rural Development Council's approach stems from a belief that "local communities are best placed to identify their needs and propose solutions (Network News, 1995).

"Much that must be done can only be done locally. Local communities have a key role to play" (John Gummer, Secretary of State for the Environment, 1994). Bottom-up decision-making lies at the opposite pole to top-down thinking. Grassroots, ground-level or bottom-up action centres on the notion of locally articulated, controlled and undertaken activities. This acknowledges that whilst outside assistance is helpful, or even invaluable, if "on the withdrawal of such aid, people are incapable of sustaining the improvements that have happened then what occurred was not development but a short-term improvement in living conditions" (Hoggart & Buller, 1987).

In consequence there is a strong argument for development as a "process which must be accumulative and must bring not just an improvement in physical and social conditions but also durable gains in people's abilities to control and sustain the conditions" (Buller & Wright, 1990). The real 'trick' is to ensure conformity, so that top-down and bottom-up approaches coincide; if the locality is represented as a Compact Disc, then top-down contributions are the CD player itself, interpreting and translating locally generated material into coherent and actual sound.

Which Local Community?

Of course there is always the inherent tension between us (the locals) and them (outside agencies); but equally it would display a form of blindness not to acknowledge that 'us' versus 'us' is another potential pitfall for communities: incomers versus longer-standing residents; landowners versus the rest; church versus chapel; NIMBYs versus developers; white versus black; young adults versus the world! When it comes to it a 'rural community' is, as already discussed in Chapter 1, comprised of communities within the community. For the would-be rural development worker that is an essential recognition, because it forces reflection on 'winners and losers', and who it is that is intended to be raised up, and conversely who may well experience some relegation. The celebrated 'Allenheads' case study (Derounian, 1992b) provides a concrete example of those who gain and lose as a result of change. During the 1980s this small Northumbrian community (population 160) formed a development trust, with more than 80 per cent of inhabitants as members; and over a six-year period affordable homes were built for local occupation, workshops constructed, tourism and social facilities initiated. A model of top-down, bottom-up interaction? Well not quite! A community appraisal triggered efforts at revival (Allenheads Residents Action Committee, 1986), and was followed by a second self-analysis completed in 1992. The latter report unearthed some comments which displayed a "high level of ill will and destructiveness which is difficult to deal with in a small community... one person's claim that 'if the clock could be turned back six years, everyone would be happy' was proved false by the majority of views expressed by others..." (Allenheads Trust, 1992). (See Chapter 10 for more about Allenheads in the context of Rural Development Programmes.) So the message is first, that change or 'development' will represent a threat to some vested interests; second, to paraphrase an 1858 quotation attributed to Abraham Lincoln, you can please all of the people some of the time, and some of the people all the time, but not all the people all of the time.

For agencies external to a community there are also fundamental lessons to be learnt regarding the distinction between localized action – for example local authority Local Plan preparation – and local community development founded on active consultation and participation with, and by, the community. There is a world of difference between passive hearing and active listening.

Why Engage Local Interests?

The first reason for galvanizing local opinions is a pragmatic one: the parish council or a local farmer may own land critical to the success of a scheme, for example, the development of a village playground. Equally there could be local charitable or other resources which can be harnessed: from builders willing to

---

Figure 4.1 *"Local people are most likely to have local knowledge – ignore this at your peril"*
(Citizen's Charter Unit, 1995)

extend the village hall at cost, to solicitors, road hauliers and other 'local talent', with specific, practical skills to offer.

Second, local people are most likely to have local knowledge – ignore this at your peril (remember the avocados on Crete!). Dartmoor National Park Authority, for example, engages local residents to host 'guided walks' for visitors. This ensures accuracy of information given, brings local people into contact with the Authority and undoubtedly flavours the experience for guests in a way that a conventional ranger would find hard to match. Chris Chapman, an internationally renowned photographer, is a guide who has lived and worked at Throwleigh since 1975. Figure 4.2 illustrates his powerful personal vision of Dartmoor. The Yorkshire Dales National Park utilizes local knowledge rather differently but just as effectively: a number of village shops act as tourist information points. The shopkeeper can embellish raw material from brochures, adding local 'colour' and detail, and at the same time drum up a bit of custom. In relation to small schools, where parents are actively involved in classes and the running of the school, there is likely to be a strong bond between the school and its community; this can be of particular importance in pre-empting any threat of closure. At a basic level local knowledge might indicate that a particular location is liable to flooding; a developer failing to enquire about this could end up making a costly mistake.

Third, is the fact that useful consultation can generate new, unthought of, ideas and thereby broaden the range of options available. Drusillas Wildlife Park, for example, has enlisted the help of interested 8-13 year old visitors to serve on a junior board of directors. Since this age group constitutes an important client group, Drusillas felt it essential to incorporate their ideas into the running

Figure 4.2 Drystone walling, Teignhead Newtake, Dartmoor.
(Photo Chris Chapman, 1981)

of the park. The results have been simple but effective, such as lowering of sign and information boards so that they can be read by shorter people (BBC Television, 1995). As an American management consultant, Meredith Belbin, has observed, no individual is perfect but a team can be. Local engagement can reduce isolation, engender 'ownership' and reduce the margin for error.

Then there is the critical importance of continuance of a project after any initial external support has been withdrawn. What will happen once the community development worker leaves or the 'pump-priming' grants run dry? As already argued "established local people are in many instances the most knowledge-able about both local needs and local resources. It makes sense, therefore, to systematically involve them not just as volunteers and respondents to question-naires, but as part-time and full-time workers" (Scott *et al.*, 1991).

In an ideal world, and in a very real sense, the outsider or external helper is working to do themselves out of a job. The Community Development Foundation (CDF), in 1994/95, urged external catalysts or 'animateurs' to look at issues from the community's point of view: "Find out and support what they are trying to do if you want them to support what you are trying to do. Help in particular the activities with long-term potential, and building up of assets and structures in the community sector itself which will enable them to sustain improvements after you have gone".

Integration

Closely allied to the idea of top-down and bottom-up activity is the importance of integration: "People and their problems must henceforth take centre stage in terms of plans and decisions" (Council of Europe, 1994).

Integrated action hinges on an holistic, comprehensive, total or all-embracing approach to rural problems and opportunities; "... the ability to see things as wholes, as unities, in which the parts are interdependent" (Dower, 1991). But this apparently simple statement covers a multitude of layers, interpretations and 'shifting sands' of implementation. At the highest level is the importance of integrated European and central government working. This implies, for example, co-operation and consensus between different EU directorates dealing with telecommunications, agricultural policy, environmental protection and so on; but equally critical is the convergence of EU and central government thinking.

In 1992 the EU allocated £109 million via the RECHAR programme to revitalize Britain's former coalfield communities. Yet as the all-party Coalfield Communities Campaign noted at the time, the EU withheld the UK allocation because "it was not satisfied that the money would reach the areas for which it is intended ... because our government set a ceiling on local authority spending it would not allow the extra cash from Brussels to finance further expenditure in the areas targeted" (Derounian, 1992b).

Of course within central (and local) government there are the same tensions: rivalries between departments and ministers dealing with discrete areas of responsibility – for the environment (DoE), agriculture (MAFF), education and employment (DfEE), defence (MoD). At least the publication of the English Rural White Paper constituted a joint declaration of intent by the Department of the Environment and the Ministry of Agriculture, Fisheries and Food (1995).

Moving on to local government, similar frictions may emerge between housing and planning departments from the same authority, or between planning sections from county and district or borough councils. The long-running 'battle' for unitary supremacy, between the local authority associations, has heightened the divisions which result, both as a cause and effect, from the Local Government Commission's deliberations regarding the future administration of Shire counties in England. The Association of District Councils did not mince words in claiming that "so long as County Hall can interfere and over-rule Town Hall, genuine local self government is impossible to achieve" (ADC, 1990). The County Councils' Association hit back in measured tones: "Local authorities based on a further evolution from the counties would be most likely to ensure local government's future vitality and effectiveness . . ." (ACC, 1992). The permutations for continuing aggravation are therefore considerable (although a single representative local government association came into effect in 1997).

If agencies are sometimes at each other's throats, then it is hardly surprising to find that their policies and programmes can also pull in contrary directions. The English and Welsh National Parks exist fundamentally to protect fine landscapes and encourage public access and enjoyment of them, but in the Northumberland and Dartmoor National Parks (NPs) the Ministry of Defence seals off large swathes of land, over extended periods during the year, to undertake military manoeuvres and live firing. Colonel Charteris, the Commandant of the Otterburn Training Area in the Borders, acknowledges that the two national imperatives, of military training and public access are at root mutually exclusive: "on many subjects we (the MoD and Park Authority) have a similarity of objectives, but the fundamental one is not possible to reconcile . . . The army needs large areas to train with modern weapons . . . such as remote wilderness areas which, of course, also attract themselves to the ideals of the National Park" (Northumberland County Council, 1993). Other flash-points might include Rural Development Areas (RDAs), and Areas of Outstanding Natural Beauty (AONBs), both DoE designations, respectively encouraging rural enterprise on the one hand and the conservation of attractive countryside on the other.

Policies and programmes, however, can be successfully merged. In 1992 the three English DoE-sponsored quangos covering nature conservation, rural enterprise and landscape issues jointly commended the production of Rural Strategies (the Hampshire strategy is discussed below): local authorities can prepare "fully comprehensive documents by bringing together a wide range of organizations concerned with rural areas to co-ordinate policies for conservation and social and economic development and to identify opportunities for collaboration" (Countryside Commission, English Nature & RDC, 1992b). Likewise the Rural Action for the Environment programme, constitutes a national partnership between government (the Rural Development and Countryside Commissions, plus English Nature), the voluntary sector (ACRE, British Trust for Conservation Volunteers and Royal Society for Nature Conservation) and private sector through the Shell Better Britain Campaign (see Chapter 8 for a critique of Rural Action). The point to note here is the strong signal being sent out from central to local agencies – we are endeavouring to speak with one voice, so you should be able to act accordingly.

The 'Rural Voice' (RV) collective is another good example of strange bedfellows joining together to make common cause. RV comprises ten national, non-governmental, agencies representing different interests in the countryside:

- National Farmers' Union (NFU)
- Country Landowners' Association (CLA)
- National Council for Voluntary Organisations (NCVO)
- Transport and General Workers' Union
  (Rural and Agricultural Allied Workers)
- The National Federation of Women's Institutes
- National Federation of Young Farmers' Clubs
- Action with Communities in Rural England (ACRE)
- National Association of Local Councils
- The Churches
- Council for the Protection of Rural England (CPRE)

The farm workers and NFU would, no doubt, disagree about farm workers' pay but remain signatories to various lobbying reports on community care (Rural Voice Health Group, 1992), planning issues (Royal Voice, 1990b) and an overall Manifesto (Royal Voice, 1991). The 1987 Rural Strategy celebrated the fact that "Rural Voice itself represents a major and successful effort to link and reconcile diverse interests in the countryside who could otherwise be in conflict with each other".

Likewise County Rural Strategies (mentioned above) constitute an increasingly used, non-statutory mechanism for presenting the strategic intentions, primarily, of local authorities. The Hampshire Strategy is a statement of policies agreed by the County and District Councils, MAFF, RDC, CPRE, NFU, Naturalists' Trust, RCC, Association of Local (Parish and Town) Councils; its overriding aim is to "promote a just and fair balance in the use and management of Hampshire's rural resources [and] to sustain the well-being of balanced rural communities" (Committee for Rural Hampshire, 1992).

At a very localized level the Peak Park Integrated Rural Development (IRD) Project, which ran from 1981-1988, is still considered by many as a 'model' of collaborative working. The IRD scheme stressed three points (all beginning with I) which it deemed critical to successful development: the Interdependence of different sectors (like environmental protection and economic development) and the consequent value of collaboration between bodies acting in these spheres; Individuality – ". . . individual characteristics of local areas are to be exploited to achieve their full potential" (Peak National Park, 1990); so uniform blanket programmes are judged anathema to localized effectiveness. Involvement, of all the relevant players within and without the village, is the final ingredient (Chapters 3 and 4 have covered these points in more detail).

Citizens are most likely to be aware, not of agencies, sectors or policies and programmes but of projects 'on the ground'. This can be a very concrete form of integration, where specialist advice and funding are brought to bear. If you look at provision for the elderly in rural Herefordshire, co-operative action is apparent. Since 1991 eight village day centres have operated on a one day per fortnight basis, utilizing a minibus and specially fitted-out caravan to deliver counselling, health checks, chiropody, hairdressing, occupational therapy and other services to frail elderly residents. The project has been backed by Help the Aged, the RDC, Herefordshire Health Authority, the County Council Social Services department and several charitable trusts. Gem Duncan, the Project Co-ordinator, observes that the mobile day centre "has pioneered an approach to support the rural infrastructure which, through its success, is opening up possibilities for extension of the original idea to include other services and other members of local communities" (Derounian, 1993a).

In addition to the above interpretations of 'integration', further constructions can be made: take, as an example, the way in which people moving to a place can be absorbed into that community. A 1991 report on the 'Integration of Newcomers', produced by the campaigning voluntary organization, Suffolk ACRE, showed that in "some of the places studied there appears a real divide between existing residents and newcomers". NIMBYism is perhaps the most obvious manifestation of this conflict. The report goes on to suggest various practical mechanisms for overcoming this latent hostility. Yet tensions between 'old' and 'new' villagers are not the only ones: the prominent and very public life that black people inevitably lead within their rural community also highlights the issue of (dis)integration. "This assumes, of course, that integration is the goal, that the process of integration is all one way... Another way of looking at it is to be concerned about how invisible black people have to be in order to survive" (Helen Derbyshire for Norfolk and Norwich Racial Equality Council, 1994). So integration is not universally or automatically welcomed as an end to be pursued, although it is generally accepted as a powerful aid to fostering rural community development.

As an 'animateur' or catalyst working alongside local people, there is the important issue of how to integrate local non-professionals alongside professional colleagues working for external agencies. It was argued in work dealing with deprivation in the Peak Park, that this should be done on the basis of "balancing formal qualifications against lifetimes of experience" (Scott *et al.*, 1991).

Networking as a Key Theme

Alison Gilchrist has neatly defined networking as "the process by which relationships and contact between people or organisations are established, nurtured and utilised for mutual benefit" (1995). Gilchrist goes on to cite the following claims for networking:

- *It engenders information exchange.* The National Women's Register (NWR), a voluntary body acting on behalf of women "to promote friendship, self-education, confidence . . . and to enable members to find friends quickly when moving to a new area" (NWR, 1995) for example, uses a 'telephone tree' so that branch members can be quickly reached with news of meetings and events. It is similar in effect to a 'chain-letter', where the network can expand rapidly from a central core.

- *Develops supportive relationships.* This can overcome a typical difficulty in rural community work, whereby action is dependent on the dynamism of very few activists. Support and practical encouragement can 'spread the load' and broaden the foundation of community action.

- *Establishes a sense of common purpose based on shared values and identity.* This builds on the idea that self-interest is a powerful motivating force. Self-interest is not meant in a pejorative sense, but simply recognizes, for example, that those living in the line of a new bypass are likely to be most concerned and vociferous in campaigning against it; likewise a 'baby-sitting circle' of parents with young children, is another form of self-help based on the shared need – to escape from little ones in order to stay sane! By contrast, there remains an acute difficulty for homosexuals and lesbians to obtain "accurate information, meet others and get personal support . . . for many . . . questioning their sexuality is a very difficult process which needs as much support as possible. The isolation of village life makes this difficult process much harder" (Shenton *et al.*, 1992).

- *Provides a forum for debate.* Residents' Groups, Civic Societies, counselling groups, branches of the Women's Institute, CPRE and many others exemplify the value of discussion informing action. This leads to a related benefit of networking: negotiating and articulating a collective view on issues relevant to participating members. Many parishes, for example, have prepared, conducted, published and enacted community appraisals (refer to Chapter six for more information on appraisals). These self-studies completed by and for local people are "a testament to the level of interest that most people show in their local community when invited to give an opinion" (Moseley *et al.*, 1996). In a different context former Welsh Secretary John Redwood, is quoted as saying that "he would not normally expect to approve closure of a school where there is evidence of strong parental opposition to the proposal" (National Association for the Support of Small Schools, 1995); this illustrates the potential power of collective action. Equally the Ramblers' Association, a pressure group committed to public access to the countryside, orchestrated a 'day of action' during September 1995: dozens of walks were staged around the country "in protest at restrictions on walking on mountains and moorland" (*Planning Week*, 1995).

Finally on this point, a recent Heritage Secretary pledged that "the public will be consulted before the Government lists buildings to protect them from demolition or alteration . . . it was no longer acceptable to decide in secret which buildings to list, on the expert recommendation of English Heritage alone (Brown, 1995).

● *It can enhance and engender the development of community-based, appropriate, services.* Credit Unions, for example, are community-controlled 'banks', that seek to avoid the dangers of approaching money-lenders, and maintain scarce financial resources within vulnerable communities (such as many former coal-mining villages). Totnes (Devon) 'Acorns', and the Stroud LETS (Local Exchange Trading System, Gloucestershire), are other forms of networks whereby people barter, rather than using money: "John delivers logs to Tracy. Tracy then gives John a cheque for 30 'Strouds'. John sends the cheque to the LETS office. 30 Strouds are added to John's account from Tracy's by the LETS administrator. In turn John employs the services of a carpenter; the carpenter exchanges his Strouds with a farmer for food. The farmer now has the Strouds to exchange for welding he needs, so Tracy gets to work again" (Stroud LETS, undated). But success here depends on consent and equity.

Another community-run venture which requires a high degree of networking in the sense of practical commitment to make it work, for example, is the community-run shop at Cromhall, near Bristol, owned and run by the village through its Shop and Post Office Association. Grants from the parish council, local charities and sale of £50 bonds to villagers have generated £11 000. "By taking advantage of the skills of the villagers, an architect has drawn up plans for the shop, a local builder is helping with its construction, and a local accountant has agreed to audit the yearly accounts. Inmates from the local prison will also be helping with the labouring" (Young, 1995).

Networking can operate on the basis of sharing 'good practice', which means simply that whatever the community's problem or opportunity, someone, some-where, has faced a similar challenge and worked out an effective solution. The 'aim' is to locate these people or projects in order to learn from past mistakes and successes, and thereby avoid a lot of time wasted in 're-inventing the wheel'. A voluntary sector environmental contacts' directory, for example, presents details of organizations and the environmental action they are taking. The intention is that, by reading the network directory, agencies and individuals "will enhance the diverse work already being undertaken, and that the mutual support that these contacts can provide will continue into the future" (NCVO, 1995).

Alison Gilchrist (1995) contends that the process of networking can either happen as a result of serendipity (happy coincidence), or alternatively in a calculated way via 'strategic opportunism', that is by putting yourself in the way of likely avenues of assistance: for example, attending the annual ACRE Rural Life conference where many like-minded rural activists will be gathering. Visiting successful projects is another powerful way of demonstrating to waverers, potential funders or other contributors, just what is intended. This idea of people seeing for themselves, overcomes the difficulty of just viewing maps and reading business plans; it brings a proposal to life. The key people behind a parish appraisal might be visited or a multi-purpose village hall could be seen in action. Personal testimony speaks louder than words.

This leads on to the related point of transferability. Networking is unlikely to provide 'off-the-peg answers', but what it can do is widen the options for progress and, perhaps, offer some guiding principles as a foundation for further action. To 'lift' an initiative 'lock, stock and barrel' is unlikely to be desirable, given the uniqueness of individual locations, discussed earlier as a key finding of the Peak Park collaborative working. To sum up: "What is special about development in a local manner is that, in many ways, it goes against established procedures. It is the place that is important, not the sector; the amateur, not the expert; differences not similarities" (Dahlgren, 1989).

Ownership
Ownership is about 'belonging', possession or control of an initiative and its direction of travel. It is the antithesis of a 'quick fix' or externally induced response where, for example, a project may sacrifice its original goals in pursuit of funding and change its 'shape', integrity and coherence out of all recognition. Ownership implies commitment, continuity and a longer term pay-off. Wide support or ownership is essential in terms of resilience and in order to increase the chances of an internal dynamic being maintained. Using the analogy of a tree the important facets of ownership can be gauged thus: A Corsican Pine, as an example, is straight and narrow and liable to wind-throw; similarly, a project based on few activists has a shallow support base, and is liable to uprooting as a result of people moving away, becoming sick, disinterested or even dying. To be effective and long-lasting, greater ownership is called for so that, like an Oak, the roots are deep and able to withstand buffeting.

There is an in-built tension, however, between a broad base of support and the danger of becoming ill-focused and unwieldy. 'Single issue' groups, like the Druridge Bay Campaign (DBC), have a specific mission – in that case to prevent a nuclear power station being built along the Northumberland coast. Similarly the National Association for Small Schools campaigns strictly within the parameters of its title. So, as one management guru has observed, "neither 'big is better' or 'small is beautiful' makes much sense. Neither elephant nor mouse nor butterfly is, in itself, 'better' or 'more beautiful'. Size follows function" (Drucker, 1992). So in the case of, say, an international operator like Oxfam, a relatively large staff and volunteer complement is called for. Whereas the DBC draws strength from its local, in-depth, knowledge and support. Depth versus breadth of coverage is therefore an important issue to be resolved. Likewise, single-minded dynamism aimed at one objective can be powerfully concentrated, but short-lived. Again the purpose will inform the structure: a campaign to reduce the speeding of traffic through a village may be an end in itself; but equally it could provide a launch-pad for further initiatives.

At Overhogdahl (population 150), in central Sweden, the momentum for an upturn in the community's fortunes began with the women, who initially wanted an opportunity to meet together. This lead on to Janter Gör – literally 'women make', a play on the meaning that women make things, make things happen, and in the process make good themselves – a three-day event with over fifty, mainly female, local craft exhibitors. As a result of this successful event, the women broadened their constituency and built up a sixty-strong village development group. They now stage a two-day community play each year, celebrating the community's unique history, which centres on a 900 year old Viking tapestry, discovered amongst rubbish in a wood store near the church. The tapestry, predating that from Bayeux, has fuelled the reconstruction of a period Viking settlement on land owned by the community. This will act as a tourist attraction. "What is fascinating, is to see a social need for company, leading to increased self-confidence amongst the women and the start of economic regeneration for the community as a whole" (Derounian, 1993b). What started out as one particular venture, has mushroomed and transformed into something both different and more ambitious. A particular success has lead to diversification.

Sustainability and Innovation
Much of current philanthropic effort is directed to remedying the more superficial manifestations of weakness and evil, while little thought or effort is directed to search out their underlying causes (Joseph Rowntree, quoted by the Foundation that bears his name, 1995).

Figure 4.3

DEVELOPING

THE RURAL
ECONOMY

**A national conference on
sustainable community
development in the countryside**

**19/20th October 1995
Stoke Rochford Hall, near Grantham, Lincs.**

Main sponsor: the Rural Development Commission

*"... Planting a tree
and then not
watering it ..."*

An image of fostering
rural action – the ideal
is not always evident
in practice

*Taken from Conference Details
– 1995 conference sponsored
by the RDC, ICOM,
CORT, ACRE and CWS*

These concepts represent two sides of the same coin: experimentation is essential for continued vigour. One of the difficulties, however, is illustrated by the Government's Rural Development Commission (RDC) becoming fixated with innovation at the expense of consolidation. The RDC will offer capital funding towards projects like the construction of a new village hall or conversion of derelict properties to workspace, but virtually no revenue assistance. This is rather like planting a tree and then not watering it! And indeed the former RDC Chairman, Lord Vinson, went further in suggesting that it is "not proper for any government to try to reverse fundamental economic trends, and it would be foolish to attempt to do so. But what government can do is temper change by softening its cutting edge" (Hansard, 1985).

On the other hand, while innovation is healthy and necessary, it must also be important to consolidate progress or achievements already made. Telecottages, whose "common objective is to promote local social and/or economic development by making available information technology goods, services and skills to economic and social groups in the local area previously with poor access" (Graham, 1992), are a case in point. Although highly innovative in bringing IT facilities to small and remote communities, telecottages have gone beyond the 'hype' so that at least 120 are operating across England, Wales, Scotland and Ireland; 64 per cent of those surveyed in 1994 "claimed to be breaking even and around one in seven reported that they were making a profit" (Telecottage Association, 1995).

Innovation remains open to interpretation – genuinely new ideas are few and far between, so the term often stands for the introduction of a topic or a way of working to an area that has not previously experienced it. Whilst, as we have seen, experiments are essential in order to foster confidence, so that more ambitious challenges can be met, there is also the necessity to recognize that "they are of greatest potential use when their central objectives include a critical focus on established organisations, and not just the spaces in between" (Scott *et al.*, 1991).

Sustainability in its contemporary sense has undoubtedly become the environmental buzzword for the 1990s. "Living sustainably depends on accepting a duty to seek harmony with other people and with nature. The guiding rules are that people must share with each other and care for the Earth. Humanity must take no more from nature than nature can replenish. This in turn means adopting life-styles and development paths that respect and work within nature's limits" (International Union for the Conservation of Nature, World Wide Fund for Nature & UN Environment Programme, 1991). A short-cut definition is the idea of "living off nature's interest rather than depleting the capital" (Conroy & Litvinoff,

1991). But in the context of this book what is of critical importance is that sustainability seeks to translate the slogan 'think global act local', into practice. And there is now evidence of agencies pursuing the bottom-up approach in pursuit of sustainable development: Agenda 21 is the local authority response to the international agreement reached at the Earth Summit in Rio during 1992, which included a call for communities to set out their social, economic and environmental priorities towards achieving sustainability.

In Gloucestershire, the programme has not been co-ordinated by the County Council alone, but by a specially formed community group working in partnership with the local authority. David Ball, Assistant County Planning Officer, has worked to ensure that "local authorities would sit round the table on an equal basis with local organisations and members of the community to discuss the issues" (Packer, 1995). These debates will continue to inform the content of the county's local Agenda document. At a strategic level the Local Government Management Board (LGMB), representing the interests of local authorities across the country argues, perhaps surprisingly, for the devolution of power "from the local authority and other government agencies to communities themselves ... this takes time and involves risks ... but the results will be longer-lasting" (LGMB, 1994a). The next challenge is to go beyond the imprecision of 'sustainability', which currently allows universal acceptance, from developers and conservationists alike, and to formulate indicators which "provide solid bases for decision-making at all levels" (Stewart, 1995).

The current chapter has introduced some of the key themes and concepts in contemporary rural community development; this is not a static picture and, as the discussion about 'sustainability' has shown, there is every reason to believe that community-articulated views and actions will gain increasing currency over the years to come. The final chapter of this book will return to debate this latter point. Chapter 5 moves on to discuss the means by which local preferences can be engendered and expressed.

Rural Community Development: 'Tools of the Trade'

This chapter identifies a range of rural development tools which can be used to address local concerns. The table covers some possible tools and highlights the fact that different tools are valuable at different times in the life of a community project. The present chapter will concentrate, in particular, on parish newsletters, the use of meetings, adult education, and 'patchwork' (village appraisals are considered in Chapter 7). Chapter 5 will interest local activists in addition to professional development workers. Each tool is scrutinized in terms of what it is, how it can be used to good effect and in relation to any potential disadvantages.

Table 5   **Selecting Tools for Local Involvement -
When and Involving Whom?**

Tools	*When?*		
	Initial Stage	*Development Stage*	*Implementation Stage*
Public Meetings	key factor	partial factor	very limited
Adult Education & Training	very limited use	key factor	key factor
Village Appraisal	very limited use	key factor	partial use
Exhibitions & Fairs	key factor	partial use	very limited use
Media & Telecommunications	key factor	partial use	partial use
Tools	*Involving Whom?*		
	Local Leaders	*Organizations/ interests*	*General Public*
Public Meetings	key factor	key factor	key factor
Adult Education & Training	very limited use	key factor	key factor
Village Appraisal	very limited use	key factor	partial use
Exhibitions & Fairs	key factor	key factor	key factor
Media & Telecommunications	key factor	key factor	key factor

After Moseley & Cherrett, 1993

Parish or Community Newsletters

Parish newsletters are general information sheets produced for the community, by the community. In terms of rural development, a newsletter can achieve several benefits. The first is the dissemination of information regarding births, deaths and marriages. This can engender a sense of identity and an understanding of family connections within the village. There can also be advertisements for local businesses – the shop, builder, electrician, hotel, pub, surveyor – which, in turn, can encourage the local economy, with payment remaining in the locality rather than leaking outside. If the community is unable or unwilling to support its own then the service will fold. Information is also essential in order to promote the integration of newcomers and longer-standing members of a community. Some newsletters even include a directory of local services and useful numbers (parish and district councillors) which can be delivered annually with the newsletter or given specifically to newcomers on arrival.

The spread of information can foster participation. Knowledge of events is critical if people are going to support them; village fêtes, fund-raising ventures, children's assemblies, pantomimes, village 'clean-ups', sports and social clubs, all must be publicized in order to attract audiences and supporters. The newsletter can help village organizations to plan events which do not clash. It may not be 'fool-proof', but can assist in avoiding some collisions. Newsletters are normally produced monthly, so that people have reasonable advance notice of coming attractions and can plan accordingly. A basic requirement is to provide information on the time, place, purpose, any cost or other restrictions (e.g. an outing for pensioners only), duration, contact names and details, who is speaking and so on. Information, via the medium of a newsletter, is a basic building-block for community activity.

'News' can, for example, take the form of details regarding contentious development proposals by describing who is behind a scheme, the site and scale of intended building work. The newsletter can therefore act as a democratic medium, providing locally relevant information direct into people's homes. The avidly read details of births, deaths and marriages do not just form an historical document, describing at some point in time who is 'the community'. The information can also trigger informal community care: a neighbour has just been widowed – can she be helped? A single parent has to go in for an operation, can anyone mind her child? A couple is about to get married – they both come from families that have lived in the village for generations – here is a chance for general community celebrations. Information can trigger self-help.

A newsletter should be inclusive, that is non-sectarian in its coverage, as opposed to expressing only church news and opinions, or those of a political party. The latter may well be of value, but the newsletter should seek to be open, non-partisan, 'factual' and balanced in its coverage. Otherwise subscribers might withdraw support for the newsletter in particular and, as an extension, for some or all of the events promoted in its pages. On the other hand some church news-letters do undoubtedly double as more general information sheets. The question of inclusion relates as much to the process of production as to the end product itself. In this sense a newsletter is a direct analogy or parallel of rural community development itself which, as noted in the last chapter, comprises the two components of process and product.

So what is usually included in a newsletter? The bulk of the 'copy' will be in the form of articles or contacts; a parish council report, a feature on an aspect of local history, biography of a village character, brief summaries of WI, Young Farmers' or other recent meetings, including the gist of what guest speakers said, the district and county councillors' feedback on matters relevant to the community. There may also be notices of forthcoming events, elections for office such as treasurer to the play group or chair of the WI. It is essential to have a willing band of 'stringers' – society and club representatives who regularly send in articles for inclusion – otherwise the newsletter runs the risk of becoming boring or repetitive in content and ultimately, like so many village services, liable to collapse, on account of too few active supporters.

So who delivers the news? Prime responsibility rests with the editor(s). They need to command support and acceptance from the community otherwise the newsletter will fail. But an editor in turn relies on volunteers to assemble and deliver the paper from house to house.

Problems with Newsletters

A central issue for any newsletter producer is, unsurprisingly, money and how to pay for production costs, materials, printing, petrol or other incidental expenses. Advertising is one avenue that offers the attraction of receiving a few larger payments than individual subscriptions, and which has the added benefit of encouraging local residents to utilize local companies. This relates back to the issue of sustainability and the importance of maximizing use of local resources. Advertising or subsidy does mean that the newsletter only carries a nominal charge or may even go free to all households.

Good quality graphics and pictures are invaluable if the magazine is to hold readers' attention. Here is an opportunity to include professional and amateur artists in the production process, thereby leavening the result, broadening the range of ownership and using individual skills for specific effect. One of the biggest problems with newsletters is the fact that people receive them and then either don't read them, or read and instantly forget. As a development worker or village activist organizing an event and wanting a good turnout, you need to use other means of publicity to reinforce your message – reminder notes dropped through letter-boxes, notices in the village post office and so on.

It is essential that a newsletter should be broadly based and not just the vehicle of one person with a 'bee in their bonnet'; the latter scenario might be termed the 'Linda Snell' syndrome (she is the Ambridge busy-body in the radio 'soap' the 'Archers'). Self-aggrandisement, jealousy and destructive cliquishness can erode any sort of communal effort. Allied to this is the question of succession: who will pick up the reins if the editor is ill or moves on? It is essential to have a deputy or understudy/apprentice. In this way continuity can be assured and the membership widened.

Meetings

Whilst newsletters provide one means of disseminating information, in a passive sense through people's front doors, meetings of various types require more active participation. You have to attend to contribute and influence. What are some of the reasons to meet? Consultation with local people is important, and may be legally necessary, for example in relation to recommended school closure. A county or unitary council will need to assess local opinion, and equally village bodies like a parish council may use a meeting in order to claim a mandate for action.

Presentation of proposals is another reason for meeting so that, for example, a developer can allay fears, explain their side of the story, and perhaps influence local opinion by offering some form of planning 'gain' – perhaps a commitment to incorporate a play area into a housing scheme. The local highways authority (county/unitary council) might also use the opportunity to give the reasons for road widening or pedestrianization. Meetings can facilitate feedback or report on progress on fund-raising, project development or, as an example, the findings of a parish appraisal and how to translate aspirations into practice (see Chapter 7 for more details about appraisals).

A gathering can also generate solidarity and articulate common cause: a meeting to protest against a planning application, open-cast quarrying, re-routing a bus service. Meetings may provide a gauge of how widespread concerns are, how many and in what ways people are willing to participate in any subsequent response, and begin the process of establishing committees, working groups or other appropriate mechanisms through which to act. Then there is the question of who a meeting is aimed at. Is it an open meeting, with people walking in off the street, and potentially with the press present? Or is it a closed meeting for WI, Young Farmers or other specified members only? Even a restricted gathering, such as a town/parish council meeting, can accommodate public contributions, for example, via a 'democratic half-hour' at the start or finish of a council meeting, during which constituents are able to raise matters of concern which may then be addressed in the body of the meeting.

How can a meeting foster involvement in relation to rural community development? First, it is essential to set down a clear purpose: who is the meeting for and what is it about. Publicity is essential, for example via the newsletter, on notice boards, in the post office, or roadside markers on the approach to the village, if you expect anyone to turn out! This includes a clear statement of the time and place of the meeting.

It is necessary to ensure that there is no clash with other big events in the community, which could reduce attendance because of split loyalties. On the other hand it can be a very effective means of reaching out to people by 'piggy-backing' on an established crowd-puller like the village fête, a community street party, Christmas panto or school assembly. Obviously the host must be aware of, and agree to, any additional gathering but by so doing you can increase the chances that people will be aware of, and perhaps will support, an initiative.

There is then the issue of where you stage a meeting; 'neutral space' may be an important consideration in order to maximize your intended audience. When there was discussion about the establishment of a Telecottage for the North Tyne area of Northumberland in the early 1990s, doubts were expressed about basing this community IT centre in a school. People might not feel comfortable, they could be uncertain about opening hours, and the school itself was awkwardly placed at the edge of Bellingham village. Church premises may also dissuade some people from attending, on account of differing beliefs, a fear of some hidden religious message or perhaps just uncertainty as to precisely who could attend.

The importance of an effective chairman cannot be over-stated. Competent chairing of a meeting entails refereeing, gaining acceptance by the assembly, not being partial in any summary or proposal for action, striking the balance between allowing people to speak out and not allowing the proceedings to drag on, or for them to be hijacked by a few vociferous individuals. A meeting should, as far as possible, be drawn to a conclusive end. Accurate note-taking or agreed 'minutes' provide an historical record of who said what and of any approved action. Advance notice, wherever possible, increases the likelihood of attendance. Timing is important since it would be pointless, for example, trying to influence the content of a district-wide Local Plan, after the statutory consultation period. Likewise, local feeling might run high at a point which doesn't neatly fit with a scheduled cycle of meetings, so flexibility may need to be exercised in order to stand the best chance of influencing an outcome. A pre-election period can provide an especially fertile 'window of opportunity' during which to squeeze out promises or consideration from prospective politicians.

Meeting Problems or Problem Meetings

Picture what happened at the border village of Rothbury in the Cheviot hills. The year was 1990. What should have been an open and constructive discussion about how to develop tourism appropriately, degenerated into a witch-hunt against the district council, which local people present felt had ignored their wishes for many years. So 'hijacking' can be problematic, although in the case cited, you could actually argue that local people were fed up with top-down actions and wanted to make their feelings known. There is probably some truth in the fact that people will say what they intend regardless of the occasion or topic being considered. It is useful, therefore, to establish who is saying what and why. This can be done by asking speakers to name themselves, give their status – parish clerk, ward district councillor, paid employee, planning consultant and so on – and to name any organization they are representing – CPRE branch, a trades union, house builder, Rural Community Council. A good 'Chair' will keep the meeting 'on track', while allowing some 'constructive straying'.

Action only results if agreement is reached; for this to happen discussion must be focused, otherwise it will be reduced to nothing. Appraisals provide good practical tools for local change, though they sometimes become ends in themselves or purely historical, retrospective documents (Moseley *et al.*, 1996). So meetings can prove effective but must be carefully prepared and managed.

Adult Education

People are not perfect. We all need each other. We all hold each other together, just as one harakeke (strip of flax) in a rorrou (food basket) does. Take the spotted or discoloured ones out and your rorrou will fall to pieces (Puketapu-Hetet, 1989)

Adult education is all about self-improvement and 'empowerment'. There is a classic community development slogan that conveys the intent of adult education: "you can feed someone for a day, but if you teach them to fish they can feed themselves for a lifetime". Adult education is a continuing process that picks up where formal education ends; and whereas a defined 'national curriculum' drives school-based learning, adult education is individually determined and chosen. It can range across cookery, sociology or car maintenance to full-blown degree programmes, for example, via the Open University, utilizing televised 'lectures'.

Another structured arrangement is the distance-learning course in Local Policy offered to parish clerks and other village activists by Cheltenham and Gloucester College of Higher Education. This is undertaken from home with support from locally-based tutors. Instruction can be at weekly sessions, or over a weekend, such as at intensive 'residential schools', or possibly through occasional meetings with guest speakers via the WI, Rotary Club and so on. So flexibility is one of the strengths of adult education.

Another attraction is that adult education can be (relatively) locally provided, and that it reflects local demand. Village schools or halls are common venues. The latter are close to home, likely to be more familiar than a distant town location, and therefore perhaps not so intimidating. In the mid-1980s Action with Communities in Rural England (ACRE) developed a five-year 'pilot' scheme of "village-based courses as a catalyst to rural community action. During that time, courses have been set up throughout rural England where local people learn about rural issues and decide upon positive action to take within their own communities" (ACRE, 1989). Malcolm Moseley, former ACRE Director, went on to note that "enlightened and empowered, many have moved on to practical action: building a new hall, launching a new bus service . . .". What adult education can do is to foster a sense of identity and belonging, as a direct launch-pad for community development based on local traditions and history. In the Peak Park, the ancient art of 'well-dressing' has been revived as a communal activity, and as a by-product encourages paying visitors to the area. The Overhogdahl example (from Chapter 4) provides another instance of local history and culture generating economic revival.

The study of local history, in particular, presents an ideal opportunity for the integration of relative newcomers and longer-standing residents. The latter are able to demonstrate knowledge and authority, whilst those new to a place can learn about their adopted home. This shared interest and identity can of course benefit the indigenous population too, as prejudice and ignorance may be blown away by the fresh air of historical study. A further claim, made by Confucius, is that you must "study the past if you would divine the future".

Another adult education model is provided by a Community Learning Opportunities Centre (CLOC) which was established in the hard-hit North Derbyshire coal field during 1991. This is a "multi-agency initiative and has a steering group with over 60% representation of local users. It offers a range of courses such as computing and skill-swap crafts and runs women-only courses ... using a multi-agency approach to community development has enabled initiatives to be established in the coal field as positive, viable and long term 'solutions' to some of the many issues identified by local people" (Eames, 1993). Similarly, the Workers Educational Association (WEA) has a tradition of encouraging self-help through adult education.

Then there is the University of the Third Age, an informal series of locally motivated and 'tutored' classes run by and for older people. In one Northumberland village for example, senior citizens met socially and to learn Russian from a retired language teacher (the 'third age' follows on from childhood and adulthood).

More conventionally, perhaps, many schools have dedicated Community Tutors. These staff encourage the wider use of school premises – swimming pool, badminton hall, sports field – and stage adult classes in life, social and hobby skills. So rural adult education parallels the approach of community development, in seeking to motivate individuals to take control of their own destinies. Often this process can be directed and accelerated by a 'patch worker'.

Patchwork

Francis and Henderson (1992) identify three approaches to community work practice in rural areas: working from a distance; focused, indirect work; direct community work.

They go on to stress the fact that agencies and workers are likely to move between different parts of this model over time, and to combine different parts at the same time. Working from a distance "recognises that all communities have needs, and that the agency/or worker has a duty to help all of them at some point" (Francis & Henderson, 1992). Focused, indirect action means that the "practitioner engages with a limited number of communities, and people within communities, on a number of issues and over a period of time" (Francis & Henderson, 1992). Direct community work, by contrast, necessitates the worker becoming fully immersed in a community. All of these approaches are relevant to the conduct of patchwork. In relation to community development, patchwork is about binding together disparate threads to produce a coherent basis for action. So it follows that a patchworker is someone "available to support and stimulate local effort. Patchworkers are not specialists – they are concerned with a broad spectrum of social and economic (and often environmental) matters, with problem-solving and with inter-agency collaboration" (Clark, 1985). Other descriptions of patchwork relate to the fulfilment of an intermediary function, a go-between or junction-box bridging the concerns of local people and the capacity for external agencies to respond to issues raised. Community 'glue' is another description of the patchworkers' ability to bring different interests together. Patchworkers or field officers may be local volunteers or 'amateurs'; but most are paid, on a contract basis, to act on behalf of communities for a fixed term.

A patchworker may have a geographical remit: for example, the East Fellside and Alston Moor Project Officer operated in just 32 parishes in East Cumbria from 1980-85. Alternatively there could be greater coverage, of a district council area or even a Rural Development Area (RDA) or AONB. The Suffolk RDA, for example, spans three districts: Mid Suffolk, Waveney and Suffolk Coastal. Equally a patchworker can have a topic focus to promote the availability of affordable housing – a so-called 'broker' – acting between communities with a clearly stated need and housing associations plus other providers. Rural transport brokers act similarly to develop community buses, car sharing and post buses. As a final example, co-operative development workers encourage community-based businesses – telecottages, food processing or even the creation of credit unions. Whether patchwork is geographically or topically based, the intention is in essence the same: to act with and for local communities.

The Bishop of Dorchester has referred to clergy as 'Religious Community Development Officers', leading their congregations as a team captain might, to engage with the wider community in regeneration schemes (Russell, 1986). In Stainforth, a large mining village near Doncaster, the Catholic Priest has been the motivating force in 'Stainforth Together', a charity which draws in elected officials, churches, social services, youth and community workers and local people all pulling together to get the community back on its feet. To all intents and purposes the priest is a patchworker, and as such propounds an essential truth of community work – the art of camouflage or invisibility: "The church tries not to duplicate anything that other people can do better . . . in most cases I'm supporting not leading. If you're doing a job right, people stop thinking of you as 'the whatever' – they see me as Joe Long first, the parish priest second." (Rural Development Commission, 1994/95)

The patchworker is the 'stylus', where the local community is the record, and outside agencies the record-player; the point at which top-down can productively meet bottom-up development to generate harmony.

Many agencies like the Civic Trust Regeneration Unit have employed project officers in places such as Brigg, Amble and Wirksworth. Why? They can fulfil a number of roles: as 'friend at court' – a person who knows the system well enough to engage with it and bring some influence to bear. A patchworker can provide a fresh pair of eyes, in order to escape from the vicious circle of decline and demoralization, so that new possibilities are raised and explored. He or she can gain from the fact that they may be an 'outsider', not tarred by local connections, family background or political ties or intrigue that can dog or destroy a worker from the outset. They have the opportunity to demonstrate political neutrality. Niall Fitzduff, of the Northern Ireland Rural Community Network, notes how community work in the Province has "found some acceptability in occupying the space between paramilitary activity and official politics. It therefore walks a tightrope, sometimes being sidelined by the latest atrocity but mostly fulfilling an important and legitimate support for community life" (Henderson & Francis, 1993). This extreme example is testimony to the tact, diplomacy and honesty demanded of patchworkers.

Community development officers are dedicated, paid workers, complementing and co-ordinating volunteer input. They have the time, the remit and the job specification to make it their business to work alongside local people. They may well be 'semi-detached', that is not tied to any (local authority) hierarchy. Such an arms-length relationship means that a patchworker is less likely to be pigeon-holed, as being at a particular grade or level, and cannot therefore be so easily dismissed or fobbed off.

If the main task is to work alongside local people, then how can this be achieved? First by working via existing mechanisms and authorities both within and outside the community – WI, parish, district, unitary and county councils, PCC, Young Farmers, NFU, Countryside Employment Programme. This includes essential and good working relations with elected councillors and their paid officers. Since it is highly likely that the patchworker is part-funded by organizations like the RDC, Countryside Commission, county and unitary councils, this opens up the possibility of 'leverage' – someone already on the 'inside track' extracting grant aid or help in kind for projects, from these agencies. Knowing 'the system' and being able to make it work to your advantage is a pre-requisite of the job, and fits with the managerial view of society (see Chapter 1), that there are 'gatekeepers' who control access to information and decision-making. The patchworker can effectively open those gates that might otherwise remain firmly shut.

A specific threat or issue – school closure or affordable housing – can provide the entrée for patchworker involvement. This legitimate contact point may lead to further activity, continued dialogue and good practice networking. As community members gain confidence and achieve results so they are able to share insights with other would-be community developers. Alternatively, a specific threat or issue can lead direct to further community activities undertaken without intervention from a patchworker. A case in point is that of a successful campaign, whereby residents prevented "Upton St.Leonards being swallowed by Gloucester city" (USCAN, 1991), and encouraged the campaign group to undertake a much wider-ranging community appraisal. This is in the spirit of a patchworker being an assistant and not some sort of crutch without which the community keels over.

Of course patchwork is not a wonder cure or universal panacea, and it certainly does have its inherent dangers. First is the problem of the patchworker being seen as an 'outsider', or someone imported to 'keep an eye' on the natives. This requires sensitivity and tact on the part of the officer, in the same way that a newcomer has to tread the fine line between sociability and not being labelled a busybody or 'take-over' specialist. The other side of this coin is the suspicion or fear that may be expressed, in particular by local authorities who are afraid of raising expectations only to dash them; people rapidly see through any pretence at consultation if it remains simply a 'talking shop'. So organizations may well be concerned that locally generated ideas and projects will have potential resource implications. This is against the uncertain backdrop of privatizing council services, local government reorganization and public expenditure cuts. Not unreasonably, councils do not want to be seen to be encouraging local action with one hand, only to stifle it with the other.

Another issue relates to the fact that many patchworkers are relatively poorly paid and on fixed-term posts of between 1 to 3 years. This poses two difficulties: first, for the employee, who must seek job security or an extension, virtually from day one, or alternatively be looking elsewhere for another post. This may well require the officer to scrabble around for funding to ensure that the position continues. At the very least this is an unwelcome distraction, and at worst can become an all-consuming preoccupation. For the employer, though, there is the necessity to demonstrate value for money and the visible 'success' of the post via projects on the ground. This is a tall order for anyone employed over a three-year period: in year one you are acclimatizing; during the second year you pull out all the stops; and by year three you are obsessed with the next step and, maybe, winding up the project.

Allied to the above is the difficulty for patchworkers to act as persuaders without a constituency. The down-side of being semi-detached and not easily pigeon-holed within a hierarchy is that it can be a lonely vigil. Patchworkers require careful support, perhaps through an informal project 'steering group', or regular contact and advice from others in allied occupations such as an RCC countryside officer or Director. Yet the officer may have too many topics or too great an area to cover effectively, or to ensure appropriate delivery, so it may end up that those communities which can shout loudest monopolize the services of the patchworker at the expense of more needy, fatalistic or less articulate places. Funding questions will constantly be asked by part-financiers: the Rural Development Commission, county and district councils, the TEC and others all have their own remits and will want to ensure that the officer is providing good value for money. Again, the patchworker has to develop the skills of being a slave to many masters, keeping all the balls in the air and pleasing all the people most of the time! Consensus, compromise and conciliation all go with 'the patch'.

Apart from tangible results – a community-run shop here, a farm tourism association there – how do you quantify empowerment? In the final analysis it is rather like a belief in God – it requires an act of faith and commitment. Patchwork and rural community development are long-term undertakings, not suited to quick political fixes. This does not mean that empowerment cannot be demonstrated, but rather that it can only be inferred: in relation to parish appraisals and their practical results for example, empowerment can be suggested by the fact that action groups have been formed to enact appraisal recommendations; individuals have undertaken related work; a new sense of identity, belonging and 'community' has been expressed by a number of parishes post-appraisal; and finally there are instances of appraisal activists being elected to their parish council (for more information see Chapter 7). Of course a specific and practical project itself can provide the key to community development, the project (or product) emerging from a process of active local participation.

The ultimate challenge for the patchworker is to ensure 'sustainability', life after the initial funding ceases. This of course presupposes that the work is still wanted and perceived as needed by the local population. The community development worker has a difficult and subtle role to fulfil by offering help and support, instilling confidence, power and ownership to a community, and then leaving at such a time that the community can survive without him. In some instances, agencies have absorbed aspects of patchwork into their mainstream operations. Alternatively a community (or more than one) may establish a development trust to carry the work forward. Community development workers burn bright for a few years and then, before demoralization and fatigue set in, they must pass on the torch . . .

Chapter 6

Sheepscombe:
A Gloucestershire Village Dissected

by Elisabeth Skinner

Sheepscombe – the very name of this Gloucestershire village conjures up an image of the countryside where sheep graze peacefully on rolling hills. But what lies beneath this pleasing pastoral picture in the valley glimpsed by visitors? Is it an expensive housing estate for the middle classes? Is it just a dormitory where people sleep at night and vanish during the day? Does a spirited community live there, enjoying the best of everything? Or is it something else again?

You will discover some of the answers to these questions, a few clues and a handful of impressions, on a first visit to the village, but you will need to explore the community in more depth to be most effective. Can the outsider rely on established stereotypes of village people? Will locals explain everything you need to know? How does the community operate and what help, if any, does Sheepscombe need? This chapter uses considerable local knowledge to identify the fine grain of detail which helps you to understand how a particular local community ticks at the end of the twentieth century. If you are to be effective in a rural community, you should take advantage of everything that such local knowledge can offer.

This chapter identifies key 'actors' and characteristics, looks at divisions in local society which are not always obvious to the naked eye and suggests ways in which the community can be approached. It stresses the value of community development practice, even or especially, in a village which already has many advantages. Sheepscombe is an example of an insider's perspective on a rural community. Like all villages it has its own distinctiveness and may be quite different from the communities of your experience. On the other hand you will find that Sheepscombe is characteristic of common themes that you will discover in other locations.

About 500 people live in Sheepscombe where groups of houses are scattered along the sides of a Cotswold valley five miles from Stroud. The settlement began

Figure 6.1   Sheepscombe, August 1983, showing the south-facing side of the valley with its scatter of houses. The Laurie Lee cricket field is at the top of the photograph. The field in the centre has now been developed for three executive houses.

as an outlying hamlet of the larger village of Painswick to the south-west. Despite its modern character as a distinct community separated from its parent village by a mile or two of empty sloping fields and narrow lanes, Sheepscombe is only a ward of the civil parish served by Painswick Parish Council.

Like all communities in the Stroud valleys Sheepscombe has an industrial past. In the seventeenth, eighteenth and early nineteenth centuries workers came and built their cottages, making a living on the back of Stroud's clothmaking industry. In the 1830s local business collapsed and people left in droves to find work in other places, from neighbouring Slad to London and the Americas. Between 1831 and 1921 the population plummeted from 801 to 383 as people moved away; more than fifty dwellings were empty in 1841 and many of them fell into ruin and disappeared. The 300 to 400 people who stayed scraped a living from rough agricultural land and farm-related trades. Sheepscombe was never a closed village protected by an estate and, since the failure of cloth manufacture in the 1830s, it has been quite unable to support the majority of its youngsters.

Middle-Class Real Estate?

The arrival of middle-class people with money seeking a beautiful place to live is also nothing new. The first known person to retire to the village was a breeches maker from London returning in 1868 to his native county. By the end of the nineteenth century the people whom Howard Newby (1985) calls "faintly intellectual and artistic in their pursuits" were finding their way to Sheepscombe to escape the rat race of London and other cities. Local builders began to thrive and derelict cottages were resurrected.

Since the last war, farming in the village itself has collapsed and car ownership has helped to suck the life out of village businesses and services. People no longer arrive looking for work; they come because they want to live in the countryside, and can afford to make that choice. Demand for country living has placed such a high value on property that the village appears to be "a piece of middle class real estate" (Silvester, 1995).

The internal village economy in the 1990s has dwindled to a few pockets of activity here and there. The pub provides part-time work for local youngsters, many of them students, while the primary school flourishes too, offering a smattering of jobs from cleaner to headteacher. Ancillary posts are hard to fill as low wages are offered for difficult or unrewarding work demanding daily commitment. The local beechwoods, owned by the National Trust since 1989, provide a little work, but the two remaining farms in the valley seldom employ anyone outside the family. There is no manufacturing industry, there are no

Figure 6.2   The last shop in Sheepscombe closed in April 1985
(Photo Shirley Williams, mid-1970s)

shops, just a post office two half days a week, while electricians and plumbers are hard to find. The blacksmiths, the wheelwright's workshop, the cider mill and malt houses, the bakeries and village stores, the motor repair garage and numerous farm buildings have all been turned into houses. For most residents, Sheepscombe is a place to live, but not a place to work.

The demand for homes has not faltered over the last three decades and people have used the wealth provided by professional and managerial jobs elsewhere to compete for a property in Sheepscombe, turning the old social structure of the village on its head. There is no social housing in the village and only a tiny handful of privately rented cottages. Throughout the 1980s property was rarely sold for less that £100000. In 1933 only 29 per cent of the employed population could claim a professional or managerial occupation – most of them self-employed farmers or tradespeople – while 45 per cent were labourers or unskilled workers. By 1983 the picture was very different with 70 per cent of employees in professional or managerial jobs and just 10 per cent doing labouring work. About two-thirds of employed villagers now work elsewhere: Stroud, Cheltenham and Gloucester are all within a half-hour drive. Many of the remainder work alone at home, earning a living from creative arts and crafts or various strands of business consultancy (Skinner, 1983).

The Culture of Communal Activity

All the evidence suggests that Sheepscombe is a middle-class dormitory but are such villages really as sleepy as they sound? Despite the commuters, as many as 60 per cent of the adult population remain in the village during the day, some choosing not to work, others retired or working from home, hardly any in enforced unemployment (Skinner, 1983). Sheepscombe has a busy daytime social life as parents make contact in the school playground or at the playgroup and older people meet regularly for coffee in the village hall.

It is another myth that people who work away from the village are not interested in its community life. Communal activity is a strong element of late twentieth century middle-class culture. Although some residents choose to live in a Cotswold village because the place is beautiful and peaceful, many also make the choice because they want to participate in the life of the village. They come equipped with an idea of what a village community is. As Pahl suggests, a village is a state of mind and "in a culturally urbanised nation, those who are truly village people are those who have defined themselves in their own minds as villagers, and act as they suppose villagers should act" (Harper, 1989).

The image of rural living which seems so attractive to the incoming population includes a lively social life revolving, for example, around fêtes and festivals, cricket matches, the Womens Institute, village school and the Butchers Arms public house. As Duncan (1992) suggests as a result of a recent survey of a Sussex village, "attendance at village events . . . celebrations of universal friendliness . . . formed the backbone of most of the participants' feelings of community . . ." People expect to be involved in helping elderly neighbours, supporting jumble sales and giving teenagers lifts into town.

Thrift argued in 1989 that modern villages are 'imagined communities' based on the value which the middle classes traditionally place on countryside and heritage, while Short (1991) suggests that the rural community is simply the 'location of nostalgia'. In Sheepscombe's case these concepts are justified; they are reinforced by its close links with Laurie Lee's *Cider with Rosie* – it is the village where the author's mother and uncles grew up at the turn of the century. Observers of rural communities will continue to wonder whether villages like Sheepscombe are rural, urban or imaginary constructs, but, regardless, the external agency needs to get on with the job; it must accept the village as a place where individuals generate real community based on social activity.

Outside bodies may be tempted to treat the village as a whole. Certainly the events organized to commemorate VE day in 1995 included almost everyone and gave an attractive impression of village solidarity. Sheepscombe is clearly bursting with action. The pantomime is a hugely successful event involving all ages and social groups whose lives otherwise follow quite different patterns. The village Bonfire Night in November brings everyone to the Village Green while the May Day Skittles Match has gained an enviable reputation for fun and games and good food. The village hall is often packed for the biennial History Society Tea Party, for a good speaker, the Harvest Lunch, or Midwinter Celebrations.

Newcomers will be impressed by the variety of organizations for them to join while the active villagers are not difficult to find and have plenty of information, energy and ideas to offer. Someone wishing to make contact with key actors in Sheepscombe could start with a visit to the pub or the school during opening hours. Useful contacts include the editor of the village magazine, parish councillors, churchwardens and committee members from the Womens Institute, the History Society or Sheepscombe Society – a forum for discussion and social activity. Most villages will have just two or three special people who have long-established and extensive knowledge. In Sheepscombe the forester has contributed unstintingly to village life for nearly forty years and is well in touch with all village organizations through his work for the Village Hall Management Committee. A former accountant is treasurer, auditor or president of almost all the village organizations and has given many years service as churchwarden, school governor and parish councillor. It is clear, as suggested in Chapter 2, that getting in touch with just a small handful of village people can open many doors.

If a rounded perspective on a topic is required, it is wise to involve more than one organization or key actor. The Sheepscombe Society arranges successful social events and may in future be encouraged to debate controversial questions. Recently they were asked to hold a meeting to discuss imaginative plans for a self-sufficient dwelling designed to make little impact on the environment, but local opinion on the proposals is divided as the site is outside the village envelope. The committee is still deliberating whether to bring this argument into the open as many members prefer to avoid public conflict where possible. Sheepscombe Womens Institute is a good forum for the debate of issues, both local and national. Its members include women who have lived in the village for much of their lives and those recently arriving from different worlds. The sewing group meets regularly to make patchwork quilts but its members, who have a wide range of contacts in the village, are sensitive to local concerns and have a clear grasp of tensions in the community. The History Society has a wide membership involving both newcomers orientating themselves through village history and established villagers who have stories to tell. Tap into whatever is going on in the village, like the pantomime, the cricket match between the north side and the south side, or the dawn walk in early summer!

Division in the Community

Clearly there are many active participants in village organizations and local events and it is easy to concentrate on their views and attitudes and imagine that they are fully representative. But in Sheepscombe, as in many villages, the culture of participation does not suit everybody. The village is easily divided into those who join in and those who do not.

This division has nothing to do with outdated concepts of newcomers and traditional villagers. It is all too easy to fall into the trap of stereotyping village people in this way. For example, it is often assumed that young people who cannot afford to live in the village where they grew up will be the families of farmworkers. In Sheepscombe, the children who cannot afford to live locally are more likely to be unemployed or low income graduates. There is little actual conflict arising from their different origins, between the traditional villagers and the incoming middle classes; too many decades have passed and society as a whole has changed significantly. Traditional villagers with links to a distant local economy based on agriculture or the building trade are rare, but some who remain make a considerable contribution to village activity whilst others do not. The parish council chair and a key member of the WI are both native village women, while almost half of the History Society's committee and several key figures in the Table Tennis Club were born in Sheepscombe.

If newcomers are people from non-traditional, possibly urban, backgrounds or people whose parents grew up elsewhere, then almost all villagers are new-comers. Some arrived just a few weeks ago but others have lived in the village for sixty years. These longstanding 'newcomers' have decades of local know-ledge and experience and they too are key figures in the community. The founder of the History Society was brought up in the village, the daughter of middle-class parents with an urban upbringing. A former postmistress, local campanologist and active member of the WI and parish church has lived in the village for thirty years. The recent president of the cricket and table tennis clubs arrived as far back as 1949 when he commuted to Gloucester daily on a Corgi scooter.

So the active people are not just middle-class newcomers, although the community relies, as always, on the arrival of new people keen to get involved. Their extensive and varied skills, energy and enthusiasm, are appreciated by existing villagers who are frequently ready to share or hand over responsibility for community action. Even weekenders, like the former chair of Sheepscombe Cricket Club, may also be keen to join in. Activists are often those who can choose how to spend their time, especially the young retired, but many commuters are busy in the village too, volunteering their valued leisure time during evenings and weekends.

People who decline to join the action are both traditional villagers and long-standing or recent newcomers. Certainly some of the traditional villagers still living locally are among the non-joiners because they feel excluded. They wonder what the middle-class residents know about 'real' village life. They watch the more affluent hurtling in and out of the valley and feel that their home has been invaded. They listen as articulate activists get agitated about a new local issue and keep their own counsel.

The joining people often wonder why someone lives in a village and yet avoids being part of the community, as if village and community were somehow the same. But some people live in Sheepscombe because they love the views and the peace of their own home. They enjoy walking in the woods at weekends but gatherings in the village hall hold no attraction and enthusiastic neighbours can seem an intrusion. They genuinely dislike being urged to come along to the WI, make a contribution to the village fête or help cut back the scrub on the village common.

So there will always be people in the village who keep quiet and more often than not external organizations will not meet them nor hear their views. Outsiders may not detect that there are very few buses or that someone doesn't like asking for a lift. They might not hear that people need help but don't like to trouble neighbours who are always busy with their children. Nobody will tell them that although there is plenty going on, they don't feel comfortable with 'those people'. The visitor from an outside agency will not discover that some people find life in a village without shops extremely difficult, that people are not always helpful and friendly, that people don't agree with what the village organizations are doing or that they are unhappy with council services and rising crime.

Sheepscombe is not an integrated whole and the activists may speak for a small portion of the population. For example, the Conservation Group (now defunct) gave Stroud District Council the impression that it spoke for the whole village in response to planning applications and consultation on the district-wide local plan in the early 1990s. When English Nature proposed fencing the Common in 1995 it thought the Conservation Group had won the support of the whole community, but the Group had a committee of seven responsible to about twenty subscribing members from a population of 500. It certainly tried to establish and then represent the collective consciousness of the community. The Group arranged events when villagers could discuss environmental issues and it developed policies which were intended to represent agreement or compromise between different interests. In truth, the Conservation Group was a focus for conflict; it became a divisive element in the village to the extent that even the committee found it difficult to reach a consensus.

It is rarely possible to develop a collective view. Different people offer different perspectives on local issues and village life. Opposing interests and values are never far beneath the surface in a village community. The temporary blocking of a short footpath by a family originally from London in the 1970s generated some unpleasant behaviour. People in a community can get emotional and sometimes changes are really upsetting. In consequence, conflict is a natural state and both active people and external agencies need to be able to handle opposition. For every person who supports the clearing of scrub on the common, there is someone who disagrees with cutting trees down. If one parish councillor thinks Sheepscombe should enter the Best Kept Village Competition, another thinks it will attract tourists and too much traffic. When villagers attended a public meeting to oppose an application to turn a farm above the valley into a golf course in 1992, the farming community from the hilltops came from far and wide to put their side of the story.

Involving the Quiet People

Approaching a rural community is rarely simple. If you think a village is speaking with one voice, you may be mistaken. Even if you imagine that you are listening widely to people's views you may still have only a fraction of the complete picture. So how do you get in touch with the people who stay quietly in the background of village life? Should you try? People have a right to privacy and cannot be forced to give an opinion. On the other hand, there may be many people in the community who lack the opportunity or confidence to join in or speak out.

A village appraisal is a commonly used tool which can give the quiet people a chance to voice their thoughts (see Chapter 7). But there are pitfalls. The appraisal of 1989 was sold by the Painswick Appraisal Steering Committee with enthusiasm, people put in hours of work and the response rate in Sheepscombe ward was nearly 87 per cent. Completed survey forms were full of interesting ideas and opinions. Then very little obvious change took place and no clear policies for action were developed. The appraisal committee had given the impression that everyone's ideas would influence the future of the village but there was little concrete evidence of this. In one instance, the appraisal suggested to Sheepscombe Conservation Group that some people wanted to improve the area around the village hall, but the Village Hall Management Committee could not be persuaded to make significant changes.

Fieldworkers are often brought into a village to help address a particular issue or make networking possible. For example, Gloucestershire Rural Community Council offered helpful advice when the village lost its shop and post office. A practical solution was quickly found: the tiny old kitchen at the village hall was converted to a post office open twice a week. On this occasion some of the people disadvantaged by the closure made their views known, but only because the issue aroused widespread support. Normally the opportunity to speak out is rare because few issues attract the attention of sufficient numbers. For example, those who resent the inadequacy of bus services know there is no point in complaining as the problem affects too few people, and villagers who would benefit from sheltered housing do not draw attention to their needs because sheltered housing is non-existent.

Activists often fail to understand why other people remain unmoved by the issues that, in their eyes, demand attention, and it is easy to mistake the effectiveness of the usual tools for inspiring participation. If someone wants to know what people think they ask for views through the village magazine or hold an open meeting but these mechanisms rarely draw a strong response.

Few people in Sheepscombe appear to take an interest in the three tiers of local government. In 1994 the Sheepscombe Society invited the five local councillors (county, district and parish) to hold a surgery in the village hall, hopeful that electors would come and explain their needs and opinions. About seven people turned up, most of them Sheepscombe Society committee members! The village has two representatives on Painswick Parish Council but there is rarely an election. When it was suggested that the village should have its own parish council, a very small public meeting discussed the issue but nobody felt sufficiently strongly to push for change. The parish council means little; people have no sense of ownership and no commitment to its activities. They pay money via the council tax without question and often forget it exists.

Students of the national training course delivered by the Cheltenham and Gloucester College of Higher Education, giving parish clerks their professional qualification, often complain of apathetic village communities. In Sheepscombe most residents are content with the way things are in the village and therefore give an appearance of apathy. Issues which seem important to some people may have little personal significance to others who commonly express the view that there are no problems in a community where everyone supports each other in times of stress.

Understanding Community Development Tools
It is worrying to think that such complacency may ignore important issues and feelings. Sometimes people lack confidence, either in their own ability to influence events or in the system which fails to respond. If the key actors in the

village are to help perhaps they need to know more about community development practice themselves. In Sheepscombe the active people have little understanding of the potential for community development or of its many useful tools. They are volunteers who respond in an *ad hoc* way according to their own skills and enthusiasms. In many instances they need guidance on how to consider the views and needs of the quieter people, how to include individuals in their activities rather than exclude, and on sustaining interest in their work when they themselves run out of steam.

Village groups quickly and regularly encounter problems. The chair of the successful Sheepscombe History Society wants to hand over to someone else. But how? Nobody will volunteer. The Conservation Group was forced to disband in 1995 because new enthusiasts failed to come forward. The Womens Institute struggles to get new members because other villagers may not be comfortable with its image. Sheepscombe Society is regarded by some as a clique.

It could be argued that community development practice is desperately needed so that the community is better equipped to meet the demands of the future. It is difficult to predict but change is certain. A few people are already aware that concern for the environment could be the greatest force for change. How will the community react when private transport becomes more difficult to sustain? At least twenty cars leave the village every day taking just one person each to work in Cheltenham, contributing to traffic queues, impatient driving on the hilltops and congestion and pollution in the town. If this is to change, the few people who recognize the dangers will need guidance and more than the conventional advice on setting up community bus projects or car-sharing schemes. They need to know how to encourage others, especially those who keep themselves to themselves, to change the comfortable habits of many decades.

The history of Sheepscombe suggests that its society has experienced critical changes in waves of fifty years. The last significant adjustment generated by the expansion of private car ownership began around 1960, so the village in the near future may begin to look different from the one we know today. It is not clear where the pressures will come from but key actors in Sheepscombe will benefit from training in a wide range of community development tools if they are to meet the inevitable demands of social and economic change when it arises.

Yes, the valley is an attractive and historic middle-class housing estate with many advantages. The local economy has all but vanished but the community (or set of communities) is based on plenty of social contact. Commuters desert the village during the day but this does not mean that the place is empty or asleep. Sheepscombe is a good example of the late twentieth century middle-class culture of participation and, as such the village sometimes appears to be a single entity – but an outsider should not be deceived. Key actors may give the impression that they represent the whole of village society or know what the rest of the community is thinking, but it is an illusion. There are many splits and conflicts to be confronted and reconciled.

The main division is between the people who choose to join in public activity and those who do not, a separation which does not fall comfortably into the convenient stereotype of newcomers and traditional villagers. The people who remain in the background of village life may be long-established residents or recent newcomers but their views remain unheard and their difficulties in the village go unnoticed. Conventional tools for developing the community do not always work. Even village activists do not know how to include the quieter people in a gentle way, nor do they know how to sustain their own action when energy supplies run dry. Practical solutions to the obvious problems are important to a village like Sheepscombe but community development offers the prospect of sustained, progressive change designed to meet a wider range of local needs.

Chapter 7

Parish Appraisals

by Malcolm Moseley

Few tools of rural community development have 'caught on' so successfully in recent years as the parish appraisal. As many as 2000 local communities in rural Britain have taken stock of themselves in this way since the mid-1970s and many more are in progress (see the review in Moseley *et al.*, 1996).

England's Rural Community Councils and Welsh Jigso, the organization which supports appraisals across rural Wales, deserve much of the credit for promoting these exercises at the local level and a good definition of 'village appraisals' is provided by the erstwhile Director of Jigso, Liz Hughes (1993). "An appraisal is a questionnaire survey carried out by and for the local community. It aims to identify local characteristics, problems, needs, threats and opportunities. It is a means of taking stock of the community and of creating a sound foundation

Figure 7.1   As many as 2000 local communities in rural Britain have taken stock of themselves – Long Ashton, near Bristol, is one such community.

of awareness and understanding on which to base future community action." Note the words "by and for the community" as the whole idea is that local people must do it themselves, albeit with some help and encouragement from outside.

That key criterion aside, the nature and emphasis of appraisals varies from place to place. The vast majority relate to places with 500 to 5000 residents, and more to parishes than to any other entity, but the fact that they are variously termed village/parish/town/community appraisals (or audits) indicates the local variation. The typical stages of an appraisal are:

1. A few initial enthusiasts seek to establish a sound basis of local support.
2. A steering group is formed to decide what issues to cover and how to embark on the task. Ideally this group is widely drawn and does not just reflect a single interest.
3. A questionnaire is drafted and the household survey planned.
4. The questionnaires are distributed to each household for collection on a later visit.
5. Responses are coded for computer analysis and the required analyses and cross-tabulations performed.
6. The appraisal report is drafted together with any recommendations.
7. The document is distributed locally and to outside agencies either free or for a modest charge.
8. There is local discussion within the community and, if possible, agreement on priorities and action.
9. Follow-up work ensues, either directly by local people and/or by lobbying outside agencies.
10. Progress is monitored and reported on and perhaps 5 to 10 years later the whole exercise is repeated.

Very few communities have achieved the whole sequence in less than a year. Two years is typical, as well as being more likely to achieve the sort of 'community development' benefits that have been extolled in earlier chapters.

Although this may seem daunting to any group of enthusiasts contemplating the task in their own community, it should be explained that help is generally to hand. In England, the field officers of county-based Rural Community Councils, and in Wales and Scotland the project officers of Welsh Jigso and of Scottish Rural Forum (the alliance of countryside bodies north of the border) are able to offer technical assistance and continuing encouragement based on their experience of similar ventures elsewhere. Computer software exists to help with questionnaire design – 'choose up to 80 questions from a well tried menu of 400 and add a few of your own' – data analysis and the presentation of tables and diagrams

(Countryside and Community Research Unit, 1991). In addition some RCCs, local authorities and other bodies, such as Training and Enterprise Councils, part-fund good projects that emerge.

Why Carry Out an Appraisal?

Few communities have completed an appraisal just out of curiosity. Sometimes there is a general sense that the place is 'going downhill' and perhaps an RCC field officer suggests that an appraisal would be a way of establishing what local people think needs to be done, and of generating a determination that something might be done. More often a particular event or proposed development provides the spur. For example, the imminent preparation of a Local Plan by a district council or the threat of something perceived as unwelcome, such as a speculative housing development or threatened school closure, or else a concern that one faction in a parish such as the preservation society has too much influence, may prompt a group of residents to feel that a census of local opinion would be timely. Whatever the initial motive, it is generally agreed that successful appraisals involve a wide range of local people in their execution and as objective a set of questions as possible.

What is 'Success'?

Most protagonists of appraisals at the local level will see action on the ground as the successful goal with measures either taken directly by local people or carried out by an outside agency, such as a local authority, in response to lobbying based on the appraisal report. There are plenty of examples of practical results ensuing; some are given in case studies below.

A quite different criterion is the notion that 'the process is itself the product' or, more precisely, that the real outcome of an appraisal is the enhanced awareness, confidence, resolve, skills and relationships engendered in the community as a whole and/or in some of its individual members. Such community or personal development can go on to bear fruit years after the appraisal exercise itself is forgotten.

Sometimes there is a problem that outside agencies have their own agendas, despite encouraging local communities to carry out appraisals, perhaps with financial assistance. This can result in local activists becoming in effect the state's research assistants, with the community development objectives being minimized. The choice of issues covered in the survey may be skewed towards the particular interests of the supporting agency, such as housing need or economic potential, with the result that the goal of getting a good, comprehensive overview of local issues and priorities is jeopardized. Typically, outside agencies want one of three things from parish appraisals:

1. Information, to enable a more cost-effective targeting of public resources;
2. Use of human resources, with appraisals that stimulate an ethos of self-motivation, thereby saving public expenditure;
3. Legitimation, with the typical high response rates of appraisals enabling local authorities to state with some justification, say at planning inquiries, that the 'silent majority' approves policy X and not policy Y as championed by a vociferous minority.

None of those points may be undesirable as far as the local community is concerned but its members, and any community worker involved, do need to appreciate the possibility of diverging agendas.

Carrying Appraisals into Action

One benefit of having outside patronage is that help with the implementation of recommendations may also be forthcoming, but how can a more 'home grown' appraisal best be implemented? Sadly this step is often overlooked by the local appraisal committee members who perhaps understandably feel that their job is done, or they may simply be exhausted by the effort, when the final report is published and distributed.

Experience shows (see the review of recent Gloucestershire and Oxfordshire appraisals reported below) that a whole series of steps is desirable to ensure that action ensues. The following have been found to be useful for ensuring action once the appraisal is published:

- Put the recommendations into an order of priority and link them to the group or agency which is appropriate to take action.
- Publicize the report via the press, parish magazine, parish notice board and so on.
- Call a public meeting to air the report and its draft action points. Get a consensus if possible.
- Persuade the parish council to adopt the recommendations as official policy, such that this representative body feels some responsibility for their realization.
- Send copies of the report to all statutory, commercial or voluntary bodies mentioned in it, highlighting the desired action; likewise to appropriate elected members, from district councillors to MEPs, requesting a meeting to discuss the report.

Figure 7.2   Extract from Long Ashton Village Appraisal.

- Set up 'task forces' to take forward agreed action points, say, those relating to environmental improvements, within an agreed time-scale.
- Introduce some monitoring machinery so that periodic progress reports can be discussed.

Promoting Appraisals: Three Examples

In *Wales*, community or village appraisals have been vigorously promoted by the 'Local Jigsaw' campaign or 'Jigso'. This was launched in 1988 with funding and management provided through a partnership of statutory and voluntary agencies. By the early 1990s it was operating across rural Wales with two officers travelling far afield to help local groups in their efforts. After six years, about 250 Welsh communities had completed or were actively at work on appraisals, nearly all of them rural communities or small towns with up to 5000 households – a considerable achievement, pro rata greater than that in England.

There has been no comprehensive review of their success in stimulating sub-sequent action, but Jigso has reported many examples of practical outcomes (Hughes, 1993). These include a minibus shared with a neighbouring community, development of a 'community enterprise' café, a traffic-calming scheme, pro-vision of recreation facilities in a renovated village hall, the development of a village sports field, establishment of a community co-operative to reclaim derelict land, footpath clearance, adult education classes, a low-cost housing scheme in association with a borough council and the incorporation of various proposals into the programmes of statutory or voluntary bodies, such as the Welsh Development Agency.

The 'process' as much as the 'product' of appraisals is ultimately the rationale of the whole exercise, but the Jigso Director quite reasonably stresses that if appraisals are indeed to promote sustained development, it is important for the local community to be stimulated by some early successes. In other words, tangible 'products' are needed to encourage the process of community development.

The English county of **Northamptonshire** has 251 parishes. By 1987 only five had completed village or parish appraisals but a statement of county council support that year, in a document entitled 'Parish 2000' (Figure 7.3), coupled with detailed guidance material produced in association with the county's RCC and, most importantly, a decision to fund an RCC parish appraisal officer, gave the process a great boost. Forty-two appraisals were completed between 1988 and 1994, and a further 19 were underway in early 1995 (Moseley *et al.*, 1996). The process required a good deal of encouragement; the appraisal officer reported making

215 visits to Northamptonshire villages from early 1991 to mid-1994, either to promote appraisals or to support those which were up and running.

Looking back at the Northamptonshire experience the process was clearly a slow one, with two years typically elapsing between the decision to launch an appraisal and production of the eventual report. There was clear evidence, though, of a host of developments flowing from the various exercises, including the remodelling of a library, building a new village hall, revised parish council leisure and recreation policies and a variety of impacts on district council planning and housing policies. This last benefit, however, necessitated the appraisal report being not so long in production that relevant deadlines were missed!

Across in *Lincolnshire*, a partnership between local authorities, the Rural Development Commission, the Community Council of Lincolnshire and, significantly, the Training and Enterprise Council (TEC), has provided new impetus to the appraisal process in recent years. The TEC has invested heavily in staff support, the commissioning of survey software with substantial coverage of economic and employment issues, provision of written guidance and the earmarking of financial support for any good projects flowing from the appraisals deemed relevant to their own concerns.

In that regard the TEC has requested village 'Business Plans' from participating local communities, incorporating such measures as the conversion of redundant buildings to commercial use and the provision of crèches or transport to help women return to work. By mid-1995 about 40 communities were well advanced, with one 'business plan' written and a further dozen appraisal reports nearing completion; the remainder were still at work on the appraisal itself.

The Lincolnshire experience again reveals the crucial role of professional support; both the TEC's Rural Challenge officer and the RCC's Community Appraisal officer, who is also funded by the TEC, have spent long hours in the county's villages promoting and supporting the venture. It is too soon to say what long-term effect this initiative may have on the county's rural economy, but some community development benefits are already coming through. In the 1995 local authority elections, for example, a number of appraisal steering group members stood successfully for election at parish or district level, no doubt enriching those bodies with fresh and locally well-informed ideas.

Appraisals into Action: Gloucestershire and Oxfordshire 1990-1994
During 1995 the present authors studied 44 parishes in two counties where appraisals have been vigorously promoted by the RCCs in recent years. The

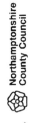

PARISH

—2000—

Northamptonshire

Village Appraisals

Sources of help

Northamptonshire ACRE

Parish Appraisals Officer (0604) 765888

Northamptonshire County Council

County Records Office (0604) 762129

Planning and Transportation Department

Archaeology Unit (0604) 700493/4

Countryside Access (0604) 237221

Countryside Centre (0604) 237220

Environment Branch (0604) 236740

Pocket Parks Officer (0604) 237222

Recreation Routes Officer (0604) 237223

Strategic Planning Branch (0604) 790888

Trees/Landscape Officer (0604) 236763

British Trust for Conservation Volunteers

(0604) 233389

The Wildlife Trust (0604) 405285

Northamptonshire County Council

COUNTRYSIDE COMMISSION

Benefits

- We gained a much needed street light
- We have more of a village voice now
- A footpath map, a pocket park, and a churchyard conservation area
- The greatest spin off is giving the village more control
- We now appreciate and protect our wildlife
- We've had facts and figures to turn to instead of relying on subjective impressions
- Useful in making representations to the authorities
- We noticed an increase in personal confidence and self esteem
- It developed considerable interest among the villagers and a feeling of belonging

Figure 7.3   Promotion of Appraisals in Northamptonshire.

Effective Working with Rural Communities

What is a Parish Appraisal?

It is a study by the residents of a village which enables them to discover the past, document the present and debate the future of their parish. By gathering facts and opinions about your village you can highlight assets, deficiencies, needs and aspirations. Based on this research guidelines can be developed to inform local authorities of the residents perceptions and expectations.

Why do an appraisal?

- To take stock of what the parish has and has not
- To assess present and future needs
- To be better informed on potential threats to parish assets
- To be better informed on what residents want of their village and for their village
- To form the basis for local voluntary action, as in creating conservation corners
- To be better able to inform Parish, District and County Councils about the village's needs as perceived by the residents
- To foster community spirit by getting people to work together
- To encourage a sense of pride and heritage among residents
- To collect evidence to influence decision makers

Why do an appraisal now?

Parish life has changed dramatically since the turn of the century. It is likely that this change will continue well into the next century.

If we are to influence change in our villages, it is essential that we are well informed of the current situation and the future aspirations of our villages.

This information can then, through a Parish Appraisal, be presented in a professional, structured way to those who make decisions concerning our local environment.

How do we do an appraisal?

Call a public meeting to establish levels of interest and form a steering group.

Invite your parish appraisals officer to address a group of interested villagers.

Decide which areas you want to appraise This could be from 2 or 3 to 22 or 23

Organise groups of interested volunteers to research each of the areas and report their findings

Analyse the findings and decide how to present them

Publish your appraisal and circulate it to all interested parties.

Review aspects of the appraisal regularly to monitor the pace and extent of change and the results of any recommendations.

Keep smiling and have fun!

The Parish 2000 Northamptonshire Pack

This pack is designed to help you with your appraisal. It comprises separate sheets, each concerned with a different aspect of village life, as well as advice on the use of a questionnaire survey and sources of further information

Subjects included range from housing to hedgerows, population to pocket parks, and buildings to bats. Although the pack is a comprehensive guide to the parish appraisal it is structured so that each parish can take or leave whatever it wishes. It is designed to enable you to pick out sheets on subjects of concern to your parish and to focus on those ideas without being distracted by areas of lesser relevance.

The pack is available from

Northamptonshire ACRE
Hunsbury Hill Centre
Harksome Hill
Northampton
NN4 9QX
Telephone (0604) 765888

Figure 7.3 (cont.)   Promotion of Appraisals in Northamptonshire.

object was to learn more about the execution of appraisals and more particularly to see how far their recommendations had actually been carried out. A careful study of the appraisal reports, and interviews with relevant activists in each parish and with RCC officers who had provided support, generated the necessary information (Moseley *et al.*, 1996).

In nearly every case it was possible to identify a clear 'trigger' which had prompted the appraisal: the threat of gravel extraction, a worsening traffic problem, concern for diminishing local services, the need for a new hall, or growth of executive housing. In 28 of the 44 parishes, it was also clear that RCC encouragement to address the concern by means of an initial fact-finding exercise had been required for action to ensue. In other cases, a newly elected parish council seeking a popular mandate or the impending preparation of a Local Plan, provided the spur.

In only two instances were the appraisals wholly organized and carried out by the parish council. More typically a broadly based appraisal committee was formed incorporating parish councillors but also, for example, members of the parochial church council, the Women's Institute, the play group and village conservation society. Typically, committees had 10 to 12 members, and most made use of the standard appraisal software referred to earlier. Response rates averaged 75 per cent; indeed only six of the 44 appraisal reports were based on returns from fewer than 60 per cent of households, thus giving credence to the view that parish appraisals are a genuine vehicle for democratic participation.

Looking carefully at the appraisal reports, 30 categories of concern were identified and it was possible to establish which were the most significant to the local communities. Most widespread was an 'anti-development' sentiment, a desire to resist pressures for new speculative development. (Remember that these are attractive south midland counties with strong growth pressures.) In addition the reports identified various 'major concerns' notably: traffic, including road safety and speeding, the local environment, a shortage of low-cost housing, and access to shops and to social activities. Of 'some concern' were the lack of or deficiencies in the village hall, a shortage of decent information on local events, poor police presence, unsatisfactory road conditions, insufficient local jobs, and inadequate youth facilities, clubs and societies.

The key question, though, was whether the reports set out clearly what needed to be done to resolve such concerns. In fact, only one in four tabulated clear recommendations or a list of action points. The assumption was therefore made by the researchers that when over 50 per cent of the local population reported a concern, some kind of action or follow-up was desirable. On this basis 400 explicit or implicit recommendations or 'action points' could be identified, an average of about nine per appraisal report. These may reasonably be construed as a 'local agenda' for the 40 000 or so people who had provided information in the 44 appraisals across the two counties. Principal calls for action were:

1. Deal with traffic related problems: reduce the quantity of traffic, curtail speeding and remove traffic hazards.
2. Improve the local environment: tree planting, less litter and dog dirt, better footpaths and street lighting.
3. Curb speculative housing development and make provision for low income local people.
4. Reduce crime and the fear of crime: more police presence and Neighbourhood Watch schemes.

Behind these 'top four' above, but still felt to be important, was action to improve the quality of community life, to retain or restore village services, renew or improve local infrastructure, to provide recycling facilities such as bottle banks, and to address the needs of young people.

However, the recommendations were not only frequently unclear, there was often no sense of who should do what and how. Nevertheless by carefully questioning those involved it was possible to establish that of the 400+ 'action points', roughly equal numbers had been wholly, partly, or not accomplished since the production of the report.

Not surprisingly the most successfully implemented 'action points' tended to be those where the necessary power lay largely in local, parish, hands. Certainly the top eight sets of most successfully implemented action points were:

1. Provision of local information,
2. Improvement of footpaths,
3. Establishment of good neighbour support schemes,
4. Creation or improvement of a playgroup,
5. Initiation of a Neighbourhood Watch scheme,
6. Recycling provision,
7. Repair of street furniture,
8. Local environmental initiatives.

Issues such as road safety, health care, low-cost housing and employment creation – all generally necessitating action by 'outsiders' – had been less successfully addressed. Even so, each category of 'action point' had borne fruit in at least one or two parishes. The implication would seem to be that some villages are better than others at lobbying outside agencies.

Conclusions

Looking at the factors which underlie the successful follow-up of appraisals in Gloucestershire and Oxfordshire, four elements were clearly crucial. If all or most were absent then very little of real value happened and the appraisal was effectively a dead letter. Critical factors to the follow-through of appraisal findings were:

- The existence of one or more dynamic and motivated individuals in the parish, determined to get things done.
- Explicit and careful attention in the report, or soon afterwards, to the process of follow-up.
- Enthusiastic endorsement of the report and of its recommendations by the parish council.
- 'Legitimation' of the report by local consultation and consensus building.

Clearly, these four points provide something of an agenda for the rural community development worker, keen to help local communities help themselves.

Looking more generally at parish appraisals, it is clear that they have become a very significant tool of rural community development and a stimulus to self-help based more on the needs of the community at large than on those of the vociferous few. Both their execution and subsequent translation into practical and useful action, though, necessitate co-operation and partnership, both within the community and between the local community and the various statutory, voluntary and commercial interests that impinge upon it. No community is an island; the key is to tap into outside sources of assistance and to know how to bring influence to bear on external agencies (see Chapter 3 for more on this point). The quality of life of people living within a parish depends primarily upon decisions taken outside it by councillors, civil servants, employers, quangos and developers, but a parish that 'knows its own mind' is well placed to influence those outside forces.

Chapter 8

Rural Action for the Environment – A Review

by Rhys Taylor

Most of the current crises of industrial society seem, almost by definition, to be located in the urban areas. Yet increasingly the shape of the most promising alternatives – a more ingenious and frugal use of natural resources, a reverence for living systems (including our own), more flexible patterns of work and livelihood, smaller, more democratic communities with a respect for the character of their local environments – is emerging out of what we loosely call 'the rural tradition'. (Mabey, 1984)

This chapter examines community development through local environmental projects, reviewing progress and experience across England in the 1980s and the government-funded scheme 'Rural Action for the Environment' during the 1990s.

A preoccupation with the issues of access to essential services, transport or schools kept rural community development firmly rooted in material concerns during the 1980s. Village and small town residents faced a withdrawal of public facilities towards larger settlements which prompted protest campaigns and a scatter of 'alternative' service provisions such as surgeries and post offices in village halls and community-run shops.

Rural Community Councils (RCCs) and a small proportion of local authorities responded with fieldworkers and modest community grant schemes such as 'Rural Initiative Funds', often commercially sponsored, in addition to their backing from the Government's Rural Development Commission. The RCCs retained an interest in countryside environmental issues, particularly through managing meetings between disparate interest groups known as Countryside Conferences or county Rural Voice committees, but such work was at one step removed from direct community development.

Concerns over equally rapid change to landscapes and wildlife habitats during the 1980s, were picked up by environmental organizations such as the Royal

Society for the Protection of Birds (RSPB), Royal Society for Nature Conservation (RSNC, now The Wildlife Trusts partnership) and the Council for the Protection of Rural England (CPRE).

Inside local authorities it was the countryside management staff and planning departments which tried to respond with Countryside Strategies and new policies within their Structure and Local Plans, but often merely describing rather than directing changes. Government agencies such as the Nature Conservancy Council (now English Nature) and the Countryside Commission fought a rear-guard action to protect the status and funding of Nature Reserves, Sites of Special Scientific Interest, National Parks and accessible common land. Development pressures came from a great expansion in house and road building in the 1980s. With the exception of land-use planning issues and involvement in the Shell Better Britain Campaign (see below), neither of these two statutory countryside agencies, nor the voluntary environmental campaigners, had much contact with rural community organizations. There was similarly limited contact with the government economic and social agency, the Rural Development Commission. It was as if rural life existed in two separate compartments, one connected with the 'natural world' – albeit farmed and managed – and one with the 'human' experiences of housing, shopping, health and rural employment – mostly not on farms.

There was a separation between the everyday experience of farmers and land-workers and the growing proportion of rural residents who either worked in towns, or who had retired to the country from urban areas. The life-long connection with nature, history and place – creating an awareness of local distinctiveness – has been weakened by the flight of former landworkers into towns, seeking employment and comfortable cheaper housing. The decade 1980 to 1990 witnessed a 12 per cent fall in the number of England's farmers and 35 per cent decline in full-time farm workers (Rural Voice, 1990a). Much of the knowledge of what makes a place special and what natural or historic features are most worthy of protection or care has been lost as rural people become towns-people, or memories die with older residents. Their former small villages mean-while grow with suburban-style housing estates to attract the new settlers and there is a rapid counter-flow of resettlement of the countryside by those seeking a rural retreat.

Local Communities and Environmental Action

Raymond Williams (1984) re-visiting his themes of The Country and the City (1975) described "a continuing flood of sentimental and selectively nostalgic versions of country life. Identification of the values of rural society with the very different values of certain dominant and privileged mansions seemed even more strong; indeed these mansions were now often defined, flatly, as 'our heritage'. . . [and] . . .'the country' as a place of rest, withdrawal, alternative enjoyment and consumption, for those whose first livelihood is elsewhere".

Although the idyll of interior decor, gardening and crafts portrayed by commercial magazines launched in the 1980s, such as *Country Living*, could be said to reflect essentially suburban values, it captured a spirit of nostalgia felt by many town dwellers for a countryside available for enjoyment without any work required to maintain it, except specialist care by rustic craftsmen. Realities of intensive animal production, wheat prairies, mechanical hedge cutters and effluent-polluted streams had scant mention. The great English passion for historic houses, reflected in the 2.3 million National Trust membership, has also reinforced, perhaps unintentionally, this idyllic view of the countryside.

What do rural communities, other than the farmers, contribute to care of the environment around them? Passive support, in the form of membership subscriptions to bodies such as wildlife trusts, RSPB, The Ramblers' Association and the National Trust, is high. Active involvement is lower, although each of these bodies encourages voluntary work parties on its landholdings such as nature reserves, or on public rights of way.

The British Trust for Conservation Volunteers (BTCV), established in 1959 as the Conservation Corps, has grown in membership to become the largest practical conservation organization, claiming to support 84 000 volunteers in England, Wales and Northern Ireland during 1993. BTCV recruits predominantly young people, most easily in urban areas including higher education centres, as it offers opportunity and transport for purposeful excursions to the countryside with lively company. Its growth in rural membership came in part through affiliation of local groups, often those formed for a specific purpose such as care of a parish or similar publicly-owned wildlife or recreation site.

BTCV is one of the partners today in a long-established 'Better Britain Campaign', 26 years old in 1996, funded originally as a competition for young people by Shell UK and the Nature Conservancy Council, and joined in turn over the years by the Civic Trust, BTCV, Countryside Commission and ACRE, with other partners in Wales, Scotland and Northern Ireland. Annual funds for community-led projects, to cover both work in progress and later celebratory awards, grew from £25 000 in the early 1980s to over £100 000 in the 1990s. Supply of information, through an informative annual *Getting Help Guide* (in 1995 the Guide was renamed *Interactive*) reaches over 12 000 community groups nationally. Rural examples drawn from dozens of projects funded by the Campaign during the early 1990s are:

- trees and shrubs for a village hall at Didmarton in Avon;
- a brush cutter and tools for volunteers managing Camel Estuary salt marsh;
- fencing materials for the grounds of a children's adventure centre in Suffolk.

In 1995 the Campaign broadened its definition of environment to move beyond supporting the wildlife site and amenity features which had dominated its early years. This involved reaching out to support 'quality of life issues' in community development terms, such as housing, community facilities, energy and transport, especially in urban areas.

In an attempt to widen voluntary involvement in care of the countryside, the Countryside Commission sponsored a series of 17 experimental projects during the 1980s. These were reviewed by Jeff Bishop of BDOR (1991) in *Community Action – An Appraisal*. These included an intensive 'Community Action in the Rural Environment' project in a few parishes near Barnsley, community appraisals, plus access and interpretation projects around Narberth in Dyfed. In Northamptonshire a succession of 'pocket parks' managed by local residents uncovered a latent demand for community landscaping and nature conservation sites – by 1995 there were over 50 pocket parks in the county. Support went also to BTCV and CPRE for local groups development, and to the national charity Common Ground for a Parish Maps promotion officer.

The Countryside Commission headquarters team wished to use its community action experience drawn from the 17 pilot schemes, to create a new 'decentralized' conservation and access support scheme, tentatively called Local Countryside Action. Their 1989-90 Corporate Strategy made reference to this: "The work of thousands of local voluntary groups, parish and community councils bears testimony to the concern and commitment shown by people for their local countryside. An enhanced capacity to encourage, sustain and respond to this widespread interest would help the Commission to achieve its own objectives of landscape conservation and recreation provision at a more local level than previously attempted. During the next two years the Commission hopes to put in place a national scheme to support local community action ... Substantial expenditure in this area will therefore be needed in 1991-92."

After repeated internal re-drafting of proposals and consultation meetings with prospective voluntary sector partners the Countryside Commission presented its ideas to the Department of Environment for approval and funding. The Secretary of State for the Environment expected the Countryside Commission to join forces with two other DoE-funded quangos, English Nature and the Rural Development Commission, to create a rural community-based environmental scheme. This was intended to address local issues that crossed the statutory boundaries for action between the three agencies.

The child of this politically desirable union between agencies, 'Rural Action for the Environment', was cloaked in typical Whitehall secrecy, and was announced without much prior consultation – in name but without detail – at the Secretary of State's launch of the Action for the Countryside document in February 1992. The Conservatives subsequently won the May 1992 General Election, committing them to see through the Rural Action programme at a cost of £3 million over three years (May 1992 – March 1995). A first step was to appoint the managing organization, independent of the three statutory agencies, for which DoE selected ACRE, RCC's national body, based in Cirencester, Gloucestershire.

Other rural schemes announced in February 1992 and launched later in the year included the Parish Paths Partnership which was essentially a Countryside Commission grant-aided delegation of footpath maintenance by county highway authorities to parish councils; and secondly, an incentive scheme to encourage care of hedgerows by landowners.

Writing in 1992 Nigel Roome, who had been a participant in the Countryside Commission's 1988 and 1990 consultations which led to its Local Countryside Action proposals, saw the purpose of newly formed Rural Action as part of a clear trend "away from elitist bureaucracies . . . setting management regimes which they or their agents deliver", towards recognition that "environmental management and improvement is a participative exercise which involves discussion and transaction with local people. Environmental action is therefore increasingly bound up with community action."

Rural Action Principles
The first policy document produced for Rural Action introduced the scheme with these words:

> Recent years have seen a significant shift away from "top down" environmental activity being imposed on communities by outside agencies. Instead the view has spread that people should be enabled to develop their own ideas for local environmental activity and have ready access to the varied resources they require.   (Countryside Commission *et al.*, 1992a)

The shift referred to above had been happening in English Nature as well as in the Countryside Commission. A community involvement policy was under development centrally by English Nature, in a tentative move away from the 'scientific expert as authority' style found in their highly knowledgeable field staff.

R ural Action is about enabling people to take action on local environmental issues of concern to them.

Rural Action is sponsored by the three statutory countryside agencies, the Countryside Commission, English Nature and the Rural Development Commission. Through Rural Action, we support:

- Action to conserve the environment and to encourage its use in ways which are sustainable;
- Community-led environmental action;
- Environmental action as a means of strengthening communities.

We believe that responsibility for a sustainable environment does not rest exclusively with Government and other institutions. Local communities have a strong motivation to protect and improve their local area. Many individuals and groups already undertake action for their local environment and should be supported in this. Enabling people to initiate, organise and undertake activities in their local area is an effective way of delivering public benefit.

These beliefs are embedded in the following:

PRINCIPLES FOR RURAL ACTION

- Local communities should be able to take a leading role in conserving and enhancing their environment.
- Statutory and voluntary agencies should actively support rural communities in their efforts to care for the local environment.

We commend these principles to all organisations concerned with environmental work at the local level and invite public, private and voluntary bodies to join in this initiative to extend resources and advice throughout rural England.

Formation of county-based support networks will bring together partners to share resources, skills and experience, and provide effective, comprehensive and co-ordinated support for community groups. Through this integration, networks will simplify procedures and accelerate delivery of support for local initiatives.

Delivering Rural Action will require commitment from all who participate. We shall:

- Listen to and recognise the aspirations and capability of individuals and groups within the local community, and respect their autonomy.
- Encourage people to take a long-term responsibility for their local environment, and to raise awareness of this responsibility.
- Work collaboratively with other organisations at county and national level in support of local action.
- Help communities to manage and maintain their own surroundings, by providing easily accessible support with training, technical advice, information and grants.
- Evaluate and spread the word about the success of community-led environmental action, reward initiative, maintain the momentum and encourage further action.

The Earl of Cranbrook DSc DL
Chairman, English Nature

Sir John Johnson KCMG
Chairman, Countryside Commission

The Lord Shuttleworth DL FRICS
Chairman, Rural Development Commission

Figure 8.1   The Commitment Statement, 1992
(Courtesy of Rural Action for the Environment)

Rural Development Commission experience of the community development approach came in part from years of association with the RCCs, but the Commission had yet to be convinced of the economic value of backing environmental projects, even if community-led. It appeared initially to be the most reluctant sponsoring partner.

The national *voluntary sector* partners in Rural Action had accumulated sufficient experience during the 1980s to convince them that community environmental action worked. They were the Wildlife Trusts, BTCV, Shell Better Britain Campaign, ACRE and the Environment Support Team at the National Council for Voluntary Organisations (NCVO), the latter only until 1994. Each had well-established links with one or two of the sponsoring countryside agencies or with the Department of the Environment. Several had inside experience of another national environmental partnership, UK 2000.

The Rural Action policy document (Countryside Commission, English Nature & RDC, 1992a), contained a 'commitment statement', signed by the Chairmen of the three sponsoring agencies, explaining that Rural Action is about "enabling people to take action on local environmental issues of concern to them" (the commitment statement is reproduced in full as Figure 8.1).

This was a bold step by the statutory agencies, much of whose work had been and remains expert-led, top-down and strictly compartmentalized by subject. It required their senior managers to make an imaginative leap into an unfamiliar 'community development' approach, previously the field of the voluntary sector and a minority of local authorities. It also involved the Department of the Environment and the Treasury in a commitment to delegate public funds through the voluntary sector, with novel rules that included acceptance of matching of grant monies by voluntary effort, valued at a daily rate per volunteer, as an alternative to match-funding. Here at last was a scheme which could be used by new, small, unfunded local groups as well as those already well established.

ACRE was to oversee the delegated funds, appointing a team of four (including the author of this chapter) to enlist the involvement of about 1000 voluntary and local authority contacts across the counties of England, in order to deliver the scheme in all rural areas within three years. The approach used was networking, by inviting district and county-level organizations to get together (as a county Rural Action Network) and make bids for two types of funding: firstly Network Development Grants for briefing, training and promotion, and second, access to the larger fund of Project Grants for local projects in their county (see Chapter 4 for more about networking).

A national steering group, representing the sponsor agencies and their voluntary sector partners, exercised quality control by considering the formal applications to launch county networks. The first four were funded in October 1992 and there were 21 under way by the following April. The total grew steadily to 40 counties by early 1995. Each county's group of voluntary organizations, in partnership with local authorities, has responded to the invitation to establish a Rural Action Network, giving complete coverage of non-metropolitan England.

What made the scheme attractive to these already busy local partners? It offered public funds in quick response to practical projects, at any time of year, made possible by delegation of grant administration to the Rural Community Council in each county. Grant aid of up to £2000 per project was available, and an average grant paid out of about £900, confirming the essentially small scale of such local action. Second, it backed a way of working which suited the existing field staff and leading volunteers in the county networks, by:

- encouraging referrals between professionals according to skills or specialisms, (personal networking), so that several advisors might help one project, co-operatively;
- paying for extended advisor contact with local groups after initial free visits (at a set daily rate) – this encouraged training, site surveys, management plans, technical assistance and safety supervision;
- allowing step-by-step development of projects at a local group's own pace, with repeat applications of small size allowed, rather than forcing a half-thought-out larger initial application as other grants scheme did – this aimed to build confidence and provide flexibility whilst protecting against waste;
- ensuring that the grant administrators were both trained and community-aware; in many cases the administrator was already a community field-worker, so that the process as well as the product was considered from an early stage.

The local projects seeking Rural Action support have been numerous – over 2000 project grants within three years of the launch – very varied and geographically widespread. Some counties have been noticeably busier, in part because they have enthusiastic networkers who made an early start on publicity, and for them limits on each year's total funding may become a problem. Local groups assisted include village hall and playing field managers, parish and town councils, youth clubs, village societies and parents associations, and others going far beyond the 'traditional' environmental groups. They may have to find other sources of finance for materials, but use Rural Action, as intended, for help with their organization, volunteer recruitment and training, public information, surveys, and technical advice.

An independent evaluation for the sponsoring agencies by Aston University Public Sector Management Research Centre (Bovaird *et al.*, 1995) concluded that "Rural Action is designed to promote a process which results in a new approach to environmental action at the local level and a broader constituency of support for and interest in environmental issues". It also achieved a "product in terms of projects which it enables to go ahead and the resulting environmental improvements on the ground."

Evaluation Findings

The same assessors however, are critical of a general lack of transfer of skills and knowledge between local groups and also observe that in some areas 'similar projects have been undertaken by a number of communities all of which have received advice from the same (network member) agency. In these counties there must be a suspicion that network members are steering the thinking of communities in an overly-directive fashion towards tried and tested schemes rather than empowering or facilitating innovative, individual solutions. "There is a need for further community development skills-training, information and support for the Network members who directly advise community groups", they suggest (Bovaird *et al.*, 1995).

The report notes that the national partnership which created and managed Rural Action "was intended to take an integrated and holistic approach to environmental action . . . in addition, the thrust of Agenda 21, the UK Biodiversity Action Plan and the UK Strategy on Sustainable Development reinforce the desirability of such an approach". Later, Bovaird *et al.* (1995) observe that "Rural Action has helped to lay a foundation for sustainable development at a local level . . . A high level of follow-up activity on current and future projects is reported by community groups, even though a high proportion of them had not previously been involved in local environmental projects."

Rural Action was not designed as a UK rural response to the Rio International Environmental Conference, but thanks to its wide definition of 'natural and human environment' helps to serve that purpose, and has been commended in several Local Agenda 21 advisory publications (LGMB, 1994a; Countryside Commission, English Nature & English Heritage, 1996).

The evaluators found that Rural Action "has already been effective in stimulating and supporting substantial amounts of local voluntary effort to safeguard and improve the local environment. More than half of all projects had involved 24 or more volunteers in carrying out the work, of which around three quarters had not been involved in environmental projects of this kind before". "Involvement in projects had several marked positive effects on the individuals concerned. These included increased knowledge/experience of environmental issues; greater understanding of environmental management techniques; greater awareness of the means and importance of managing the local environment and enhancing organisational skills." (Bovaird *et al.*, 1995)

The project support and grants, although seen by some users as bureaucratic, despite attempts to simplify the paperwork, had a good reputation amongst community groups. Bovaird *et al.* (1995) summarize them in terms of:

- high quality technical advice,
- quick response to applications,
- user-friendly, face-to-face contact with advisors,
- the most comprehensive range of funded elements of any equivalent scheme to date,
- recognition of the social objectives which many groups have for projects, alongside the environmental ones.

Bovaird *et al.* (1995) predict that "given the continuing high profile of environmental issues, [and] the growing impact of Agenda 21 ideas on the need for all to recognise their responsibilities and act accordingly, demand for Rural Action grants is likely to increase substantially and not diminish in subsequent years". In the autumn of 1995 the DoE/MAFF Rural White Paper endorsed Rural Action, and its funding was renewed for a further three years. Whether it is community environmental action at a cut price for the Government's countryside agencies or truly empowering community development will become clearer as the scheme progresses. At least it is being given long enough to find out.

Chapter 9

Village Schools and Community Development

To be effective community development workers must understand the context and environment they are working in, so that they can make informed and realistic contributions. In relation to education, village primary schools have been on the receiving end of a wave of recent reforms instituted by the Conservative Government: local accountability for school management (LMS) whereby individual schools manage a delegated budget; the impact of OFSTED inspections and the auditing of academic work; the possibility of opting out from local authority control, including grant-maintained status (GM). There has also been the introduction of a standardized national curriculum and increased responsibilities for school governors. Additionally, greater emphasis has been placed on test results and parental choice of schools. These changes represent a challenge and an opportunity for rural development.

Historically, village schools and community action have been restricted to fighting closure. We can look at the small agricultural community of Plymtree, East Devon, during the mid-1980s. Parents and governors of the primary school successfully challenged county council figures claiming to demonstrate a declining school roll. A public meeting was convened as part of the formal consultation process, at which paintings of each new school entrant created by that child, were pinned up in the village hall. This was both an emotive and effective weapon. The fight was won and the school saved! In community development terms the process of defending their school drew together the parish council, parents, pupils, WI and other community institutions to make common cause. So 'fire-fighting', or an external threat, can be powerful spurs to communal action. And in the case of Plymtree this individual experience led local activists, in conjunction with the county and community councils, to establish a Devon Association for the Support of Village Schools. So a specific danger triggered a longer-term, strategic response.

It is therefore of critical importance to take one step back and normalize school-community relations before any threat arises. As the Community Council of Northumberland (CCN), a county-based campaigning charity, commented back in 1983: "The local primary school can be a very important instrument in rural community development. At present, however, schools play this role by chance, rather than design. A continuous and open dialogue between school and residents . . . might allow more mutual support and benefit to develop." In subsequent research they went on to prove that "across the county schools are open for weekday evening use on about 27% of all possible occasions, but . . . some schools are not used at all" (Community Council of Northumberland, 1994). This indicates great potential but also wasted opportunities for close and constructive school-community partnership.

Bell and Sigsworth (1992) argue that school-community collaborations not only enrich the education which children receive but also community life. Community enhancing ventures:

- Stimulate a sense of place;
- Strengthen and extend the community's network;
- Generate a shared knowledge and understanding of the community and its setting;
- Help improve the quality of life of the community, and its environment.

This chapter highlights the three-way flow of benefits which can result from close community-school relations: first, benefits to the school itself, then gains for the schoolchildren and finally benefits to the school's host community. "The school and community should be as one. Far from simply using the community as a laboratory or allowing the school facilities to be used by the community in the evenings and during vacations, students and teachers should engage with the community at large, forging two-way relationships that not only educate, but also endure and make a difference in the quality of life" (Wigginton, 1980).

Benefits to the school can be encouraged through the following deliberate actions or 'strategic opportunism': to begin with it is important to *harness local skills* – maybe a parent who is a qualified accountant, a local history buff, someone with sporting experience, or with knowledge of press and publicity, legal expertise and so on. This reinforces the point made in an earlier chapter that individual teachers or parents can't be perfect but a team can be. It also highlights the idea of an involved community valuing its local services, including the school. By staging a *'Community week'* series of events at which the school holds 'open house' to visitors or, conversely, takes productions out from the school and into the wider community, connections between school and community can be reinforced. Written requests to draw adults into the school may well fail, whereas a subtler approach through the school cook or secretary can succeed – ". . . people get involved because somebody speaks to them, through personal contact. You start by talking to people who actually live there . . . You know who your ambassadors are. Your lollipop lady is essential" (Bell & Sigsworth, 1992).

There is a big issue to be addressed here: at a time of tight state expenditure when does the harnessing of local skills become community 'black-legging'? Parents invariably want to do the best for their children, which is a powerful motive for involvement, and fundraising in particular, but not all schools and communities have the same level of human resources to exploit. Individual school gain may therefore reinforce inequalities of opportunity and resource provision, and evidence of local commitment may well attract outside support as well. On the other hand, and in theory, self-help in one place could release finance to some-where else unable to help itself. The community development worker therefore has to operate pragmatically in the world as it is, while at the same time working to bring about improvement, albeit incremental, in the longer term.

Knowledge of other cultures can be engendered by drawing in parents and friends from diverse backgrounds, so that others in the school and village can learn about Passover, Chinese New Year and other major festivals in the calendar of global faiths. A by-product is likely to be greater awareness and understanding of those who are 'different', which can in turn reduce social isolation and exclusion. These are suggestions only and the specifics will, of course, vary from place to place, but what they do illustrate is that, even in the tiniest places and their schools, there may well exist untapped potential for community develop-ment through the medium of curriculum enrichment. 'Small' does not have to mean 'insular'.

Fund-raising can be tied to having fun rather than being (seen as) a dry as dust 'civic duty'. Self-interest, as discussed elsewhere in this book, is a powerful motiv-ating force, and parents will respond to their children's participation or perceived benefit from a particular venture. So the promotion of 'fun-raising' is important to participation. Furthermore, parish and town councils can and should finan-cially support their schools, even though 99 per cent of them will think they can't help! Local councils exist to serve and improve conditions for their constituents, so what could be more in line with such a remit than direct assistance to the village school? Parish government needs to realize that spending local taxpayers' money, rather than being tantamount to profligacy, is the only way in which their localities can be maintained and improved for local benefit. The council that celebrates levying virtually no rate can only deliver marginal improvement.

Pre-school liaison is essential in order to secure a smooth succession from playgroup to primary school and thereby to continue the 'village connection'. This can be fostered through playgroup invitations to school drama productions and staff exchanges between the two. In Winchcombe, a town of around 5000 on the edge of the Cotswolds, there is a closer connection still, with one of the playgroup leaders serving as a governor for the Infants School. That means she regularly sees her protégés as they progress through the school and can adjust her regime according to changing educational requirements for the reception class.

A high and positive profile for a school is critical to its success and survival. So a regular newsletter and press releases circulated to local TV, radio and newspapers, who love stories about children, as do the parents, are important. Every effort should be made to ensure coverage of school events – vary the tack and don't be too pedestrian in the way it is put across; is there an unusual 'angle' to 'sell'? Local media are usually desperate for a good story, so give advance notice and remind them close to the event. A photograph is especially powerful and will be remembered long after the text has faded from memory. A periodic school 'newspaper' production is another idea that might appeal to a local 'paper, where it sponsors the production and advises staff and pupils direct about article writing, design, editing and so on. Contributing children learn, in the process, about creative writing, deadlines, spelling and accuracy of information. A 'starting school' information pack is another idea that could grow from local media working with a school, and would provide prospective school entrants with background information on rules, expectations, and potential parental involvement amongst other things.

With publicity work someone, somewhere in the community, is almost certain to be skilled at writing press statements and campaigning. Spread the load though, and do not dump it all on one hapless individual who will become despondent, sooner rather than later. Also ensure that somebody is working as an apprentice, substitute or potential 'heir to the title' (this is identical to the advice already given with regard to community newsletters, in Chapter 5). Exhibitions of the children's work in the community are potent means of drawing school and community together; staged in the village hall, local shop or post office, the pub, library or even mobile library van. The overriding goal is to spread the word on the basis that an involved community is a committed one.

Partnership and co-operation within the school community must complement collaborations with the wider village community, and this should draw in teaching and non-teaching staff, parents, governors and pupils. If those most directly involved in the school are motivated, a powerful drive for excellence and for drawing in other potential contributors is generated. The clustering of small schools means that they join forces on a regular basis, to stage events that individually they could not because of too few children. An example is the Hampton (Northumberland) Cluster Ceilidh Band which consists of 20 children, staff and parents from several remote schools that meet bi-monthly to learn, enjoy and play dance music. Gym, badminton, cricket, photographic, drama and other clubs can operate on a similar basis, by gaining strength from a number of schools' contributions. By visiting other villages, their schools and pupils, children can begin to experience life beyond their own village boundary.

Benefits to the Children
These benefits are deliberately not discussed at any length because the focus of this book relates to rural community development, but in these terms, Bell and Sigsworth (1992) highlight the importance of group projects such as a litter drive: "the children who participate must benefit in terms of understanding how people can work together to sustain and improve community life". This sort of activity may incline people, in later life, to the personal and wider value of community involvement.

A strong sense of orientation or identity is a major claim made for small schools. The school is perceived as an extension of the family, perhaps grandparents, father, aunts and family friends all have attended the same village school. Roland Bailey commented in 1955 that there is "something inherently valuable for the growth of the child in being part of his native background". Lifelong friendships can be forged from pupil to pupil, parent to parent, or parent to pupil, arising from school visits, helping in class and extra-curricular events.

Benefits for the Community
Staging an annual 'Civic meal' to which all school-age pupils are invited, is the novel approach already undertaken by Swanley Town Council, Kent, so that they can hear younger people express their views on local affairs. This has a twin benefit: the Council gains a particular perspective from a section of its electorate, thus overcoming indifference to attending public or council meetings; it is also a way of trying to counter a frequently perceived sense of alienation voiced by younger people in the countryside. 'Shadow parish councils' can encourage young people to contribute ideas by acting as a parallel or sub-group of the formal parish council hierarchy.

A school is of course a modest but important local job provider of teaching posts, caretaker, school secretary, dinner 'lady', nursery assistant and so on. Local businesses and the wider community can benefit from the use of school facilities such as IT (information technology) provision. Crickhowell Telecottage, on the edge of the Brecon Beacons for example, is based in the small secondary school but open for public use. Equally Sheepscombe Primary School (Gloucestershire) allows local, paid, usage of the photocopier and other reprographics equipment.

Bell and Sigsworth (1992) contend that the village school constitutes an essential human 'anchor-point'. Berwick-upon-Tweed's Whittingham primary school wall-hanging demonstrates this in the form of a 'parish map', a school-based community project producing a permanent artefact celebrating local distinctiveness. Nationally 25 per cent of primary schools are Church of England aided, and this opens up formal and informal opportunities for church-community-school collaborations; for mutual benefit. This is particularly appropriate in the post-ACoRA era (the Archbishops' Commission on Rural Areas published its report *Faith in the Countryside* during 1990).

Schools can also act to foster integration of different sectors of the community and to disseminate information. For example, newcomers to a place can rapidly be assimilated into PTA, fund-raising, and other informal means of becoming known and accepted within their new home village. Senior citizens may likewise be accommodated in the running of the school: at Chatton school, in the Scottish borders, Age Concern operates a luncheon club which promotes social mixing for older residents, contact with and for young children – many of the younger and older people are related anyway. Thus there is the valuable bonus of generations joining together to promote greater mutual understanding and respect.

Then there is the important role of the ' school-gate jungle radio', as a means of broadcasting news, views, dates for the diary and (dangerously) gossip. So not all news is necessarily good news. Finally the school can act as a magnet or focus for village vitality, especially in dormitory villages, or in those with a heavy preponderance of second homes. The school may be the only public building offering neutral and open access to all.

For community development the village school presents an opportunity to reach and involve younger people. This relates not only to the children themselves but also to their parents (including single parents), who may be too preoccupied with work and family, or uncertain of their ability, to contribute to community action. Here is a potential vehicle for personal development and community benefit, bringing together a process of empowerment and a product of practical benefit to others.

There are gains to be had from school and local industry links. In the early 1990s Kingswood School, near Wotton-under-Edge, produced a newspaper which covered community issues such as the need for affordable housing, and drew in parents, governors and parish council to be interviewed by pupils. The process of assembling the paper was complemented by the end-product. Produced at a local print works, the children were able to tour the site as the newspaper was being run off, thus gaining an insight into how this local business operated.

The future importance of rural schools as an engine for community development is intimately bound up with the prospects of villages themselves: 1991 Census figures for England highlight the population exodus from cities, and consequent repopulation of the countryside (see Table 1 in Chapter 1). The opinion poll group MINTEL, undertook a survey in 1992 which purported to show that 4.5 million people planned to move to the country by 1997. Similarly a Scottish Office 'Rural Life' study (1992) predicts that 30 per cent of Scotland's population will live in rural areas by the year 2000, compared with 25 per cent in 1971. The importance of effective village school and community links should therefore only increase in significance as the millennium approaches.

Chapter 10
Area-Based
Rural Development
by Malcolm Moseley

Rural community development has been taken in this book until now to mean a process of deliberate change engineered at the very local level. The task of the rural community worker has been portrayed as that of working with and for local people, on individual projects and at the scale of a single village, small town or parish. Obviously in any one year this might necessitate working with several local communities simultaneously, but nevertheless this has been assumed to involve separate ventures.

Increasingly, however, rural development has been seen as best pursued on a wider geographical canvas, with the needs and potential of, say, 20, 30, or 50 contiguous parishes being appraised and addressed in the round. 'Integration' has become the catchword: the integration of objectives, whether economic, social or environmental; of agencies each with their own perspective on change; and of the needs of the various local communities (see Chapter 4 for more on integrated action). A 'federation' of one-off projects, however worthy they might be, is unlikely to maximize either community well-being or the efficient use of resources, for the simple reason that everything affects everything else, hence, for example, the 'Rural Development Programmes' fostered by England's Rural Development Commission, and similar area-based integrated programmes attempted elsewhere. In this context, the task of the rural development worker is rather different; it involves working at arm's length from a local community, trying to steer or at least influence a complex technical and political process.

This chapter briefly reviews the small-area integrated rural development process, and the role of the development worker within it. Particular reference is made to three discrete initiatives.

The Rise of Rural Development Programmes
The growing reliance placed on small-area integrated development programmes

as a means of addressing the familiar gamut of social, economic and environmental problems besetting much of rural Europe, reflects a need for integration at various levels. Aims of area-based programmes are:

- To treat social, economic and environmental issues in an holistic way;
- To develop partnerships of relevant agencies working to mutually agreed objectives;
- To set individual projects and initiatives in the framework of an agreed strategy for the whole area;
- To involve local people, as well as local agencies, in both fashioning and delivering a negotiated programme.

Typically the process of drawing up an agreed programme takes several months, and implementing it several years (Moseley, 1996a). The main steps in drawing up an agreed programme are:

1. A **'baseline study'** to clarify the area's key characteristics – trends, problems, resources, opportunities, weaknesses and constraints;
2. A statement of broad **goals and objectives**, taking a five or ten-year perspective, with some targets or 'milestones' to give a sharper operational focus;
3. A **strategy**, setting out the broad measures to be taken over several years to attain the aims and objectives defined, and also who it is that has the responsibility for action;
4. **'Operational plans'**, often one year in duration, listing in detail forthcoming projects, their sources of funding and sponsoring bodies;
5. A mechanism for **monitoring** progress and for rolling forward the one-year operational plan and, ultimately, the strategy itself.

Managing such a process requires both technical and political skills. Technical skills are needed to research the area's changing circumstances, for the formulation of a draft strategy, for the appraisal and implementation of individual projects and for monitoring the whole venture. Political capability is required to unite and sustain the alliance of relevant agencies which will collectively agree and carry out the programme, and also in working with local communities, firms and individuals who will have their own views on what is needed and what projects should be undertaken.

The Forest of Dean Rural Development Programme
In 1993 England's Rural Development Commission reaffirmed its commitment to Rural Development Programmes (RDPs), ten years after their original launch, and re-drew the associated Rural Development Areas (RDAs) to which they relate

so that they now cover 35 per cent of England (Rural Development Commission, 1993a) (Figure 10.1). It also restated which partners it hoped to see involved, how the strategies and operating plans should be drawn up, and what assistance might be forthcoming from it as England's premier rural development agency.

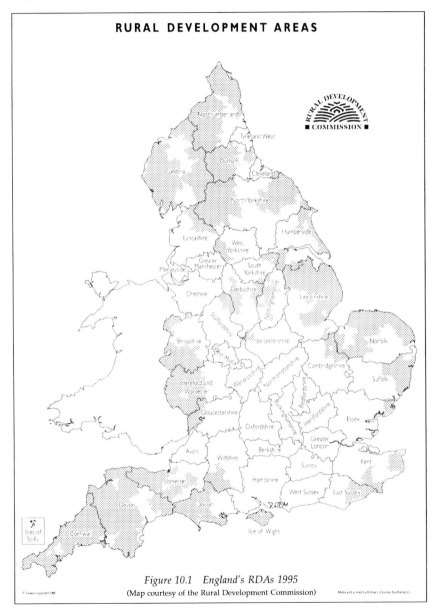

RURAL DEVELOPMENT AREAS

Figure 10.1   England's RDAs 1995
(Map courtesy of the Rural Development Commission)

The new Forest of Dean RDA covers about 500 sq. km and is home to about 70 000 people. It is a former coal-mining area, more forested than farmed, with a vulnerable manufacturing base, a weak service sector, an ageing population, four small towns, straggling ex-mining villages, a strong cultural identity, and growing popular concern for the disaffection of local young adults. The present author was invited to undertake a 'needs study' to help define priorities, and then to draft the strategy which would form the basis of the subsequent development programme (Forest of Dean RDP Committee, 1995).

The 'needs study' had to be completed in three months, so six quick exercises were carried out:

1. A review of recent literature relating to the area, including several published and unpublished sectoral studies or plans.
2. An analysis of 1991 census data, concentrating on 27 indicators of malaise for the 31 parishes, such as unemployment and the number of lone-pensioner households, with a view to defining the most disadvantaged places and the size of certain disadvantaged social groups.
3. A synthesis of the seven village or town appraisals which had been carried out by local people in the previous 5 years (see Chapter 7 for more on appraisals).
4. Interviews by phone or in person with 26 leading local figures in the public or voluntary sectors.
5. A household survey involving in-depth discussions with 150 households living in three contrasting parishes.
6. A SWOT analysis which involved a selection of local people spending a morning 'brainstorming' their perceptions of the area's Strengths, Weaknesses, Opportunities and Threats.

What emerged were listings of priority issues, for example, affordable housing; of priority social groups such as young people aged 16–25; and priority localities like the run-down ex-coal town of Cinderford. Going on from these statements of need was an appraisal of the opportunities and constraints which would underpin the subsequent strategy. For example, the area's proximity to three motorways and its industrial heritage, were both being under-exploited, while the 'leakage' of consumer spending to neighbouring large towns and various skill shortages clearly needed to be addressed. The strategy for the RDA flowed from all of this after a period of local consultation entailing a number of public meetings, and a process of political debate involving members of the RDP committee and the agencies which they represented.

Once the strategy was approved by the local and national parties to the process, the first year's operating plan could be put together. This required wide publicity of the strategy and soliciting ideas for projects that would help to achieve it. In theory it also involved persuading the area's 'big spenders' such as the Local Education Authority and Gloucestershire Training and Enterprise Council to modify their mainstream programmes so as to accord better with the agreed strategy. In practice this has proved difficult – in the Forest of Dean as elsewhere – with the result that the RDP has in large measure taken on the flavour of an assemblage of projects, more or less related to one another and to the agreed objectives.

The Northumberland Rural Development Programme

From 1985 to 1993 the principal author of this book, James Derounian, was intimately involved in the Northumberland RDP as its Rural Development Officer, as described in Derounian and Moseley (1994). Below the focus is his work in soliciting and championing local projects which would help to achieve the RDP's aims, rather than considering the preparation and management of the programme itself.

At the time, the Northumberland RDA was one of the largest in the country, with 95 000 residents scattered across more than 4000 sq. km. It suffered from high unemployment, a limited range of job opportunities, continued loss of population, especially younger people, and very poor access to services and public transport. The RDP Committee, which it was the Rural Development Officer's job to service, brought together senior representatives from the county and district councils, the Rural Community Council, the RDC itself and also the latter's development agents at that time, namely English Estates and the Council for Small Industries in Rural Areas (CoSIRA).

Looking back at the projects that were supported by the RDP Committee in the late 1980s, it is clear that, as intended, a wide range of organizations were involved. Thirty different local bodies in the public, private and voluntary sectors were funded to carry out specific projects linked to the RDP's aims, and up to seven local organizations committed part-funding to these ventures. However, with one notable exception, there was virtually no evidence of local integration of these one-off projects; where local synergy occurred this was nearly always fortuitous.

The notable exception was Allenheads and as this has now attained the status of a sort of national 'flagship' of very localized integrated rural development, it is worth considering it in some detail.

A small, remote upland village, Allenheads' prosperity had been based on the now defunct extraction of non-ferrous minerals and on the jobs generated by a local estate – Allenheads Hall employed 36 staff into the 1950s. By 1980 an air of decay had settled on the village: a picture of neglect, emigration and the withering of local services; its population had shrunk to about 160.

In late 1985 the RDP's Rural Development Officer suggested to some local residents that the Community Council of Northumberland might be able to help and, with its support, a Residents' Action Committee duly undertook and published a village appraisal which charted the priorities for action: services for elderly people, improving the environment, job creation and the restoration to productive use of a number of derelict properties (see Chapter 7 for more on village appraisals and subsequent action). A feasibility study followed and led in turn to the conversion of the redundant 'Old Inn' into a community meeting and activity centre, a shop/post office and an exhibition of the lead-mining heritage. Allenheads Village Trust was formed, and the late 1980s also saw the completion by North Housing Association of six dwellings for elderly people.

Allenheads was, as the Prince of Wales remarked on a visit in 1988, "a model community development initiative". The RDP Committee had played a significant role in the project, including advice and support by the Rural Development Officer over a number of years and the orchestration of substantial financial support. In 1986 the RDP Committee gained pledges for the Trust's proposals as follows: RDC £24350, Tynedale Council £21000, County Council £18000, Countryside Commission £16500, Parish Council £1300, and the redundant 'Old Inn' gifted by Lord Allendale. The same supporters and others, including what was then the Manpower Services Commission, together with various local and regional businesses, had put almost £500000 into the village by 1990.

Allenheads demonstrates the RDP process working at its best: integration, co-ordination, local impetus, 'leverage' of local cash, and economic, social and environmental objectives working in harness. But the Rural Development Officer recalled that Allenheads was something of an exception: it was generally much harder to help bring about a real local dynamic for development, or to get the various 'players' involved in the RDP to see the whole exercise as anything more than a mechanism for gaining grant aid from the Government's RDC for worthy local projects. Even at that level, the RDP process was of course worthwhile, but its proponents hoped for significantly more.

The LEADER 1 Programme

LEADER 1 (Liaison Entre Actions de Développement de l'Economie Rurale) was a European Union pilot project, running from 1992-1994, designed to foster integrated area-based rural development with the strong involvement of local people. It represented a reaction to more conventional top-down approaches to the resolution of Europe's rural problems and also an official recognition of the distinctiveness of Europe's rural districts and of the consequent need for locally fashioned responses to their concerns. Although this way of working owed much to England's RDP experience, there were only two LEADER 1 areas designated in England out of a UK total of 13 and a European total of 217. LEADER 2, built on very similar principles, is running from 1995 to 1999 with enhanced funding, and with a much larger share of rural England included.

Table 10   LEADER 1 1992-94: A Summary

Europe: 217 LEADER areas.

   Average extent: 1700 km^2
   Average population: 53 000
   Average funding: £4.2 million
   Chief foci: rural tourism projects, training and human development, adding value to agricultural produce, small firms and craft enterprises.
   Involvement: of 2000+ people in the various local 'action groups'.
   Support: for over 20 000 projects across Europe.

UK: 13 LEADER areas:
       Scotland (6)
       Wales (4)
       England (2)
       Northern Ireland (1)

   Average funding: £3.19 million.

Each 'local action group', namely an alliance of local partners brought together to devise and manage the programmes, had on average £3 to 4 million to deploy to back locally suggested projects which, directly or indirectly, would enhance the immediate economy. The largest category of projects related to some aspect of tourism, with training ventures, adding value locally to agricultural produce and promoting small firm and craft enterprises coming next in importance.

In the present context the focus is on the extent to which LEADER met one of its central objectives, namely putting local people and organizations at the centre of the decision-making process (Moseley, 1996b).

Effective Working with Rural Communities

This was urged for two reasons: first, to try to ensure respect for the diversity of the circumstances, problems and resources of rural Europe; second, to help establish a people-centred process of rural development, with local people 'learning by doing' – developing their awareness, confidence and skills by means of genuine involvement in the rural development programme. The most obvious way of achieving this was to involve appropriate people in the management partnerships and – more difficult – to ensure that this was a learning experience.

Some of the management partnerships were established as 'mixed economy' companies; some as not-for-profit organizations, others were in effect offshoots of public sector bodies. In France, for example, inter-communal 'syndicates' tended to play a significant role, while in the seven Scottish LEADER programmes, the key players were the Local Enterprise Companies.

Taking a European perspective, the most frequent members of these local groups were the local authorities and other public organizations with a relevant remit, for example, Tourist Boards and Regional Development Agencies, private companies including banks and agricultural co-operatives, voluntary bodies from the social and cultural spheres, and professional and trade organizations. Assuming that at least ten such bodies were involved in each of the local groups, then across Europe at least 2000 local or regional bodies were actively involved in determining and delivering locally focused rural development programmes. The 'learning process' implied by this participation may prove, in the long run, to be a very significant factor in shaping rural Europe.

In order to involve the wider public, the Brussels-based LEADER Co-ordinating Unit published some early advice covering the why, when, who and how of local popular involvement (Moseley & Cherrett, 1993). Briefly reviewed were the merits and limitations of community development workers, local networks and forums, co-operatives, public meetings, adult education initiatives, village appraisals, exhibitions and fairs, the local media and telecommunications.

Although there is no comprehensive evidence about the subsequent use of such techniques, there are some striking examples of success, including the establishment of 'citizen's committees' for each locality in the Terre del Socio area of Sicily. These Sicilian local groups drew up their own integrated development programmes to be considered alongside the recommendations of 'sectoral committees' of professionals covering tourism, agriculture and small businesses across the whole area. The goal was to break with the area's tradition of dependency and fatalism and the resigned expectation that financial aid would always go to favoured protégés.

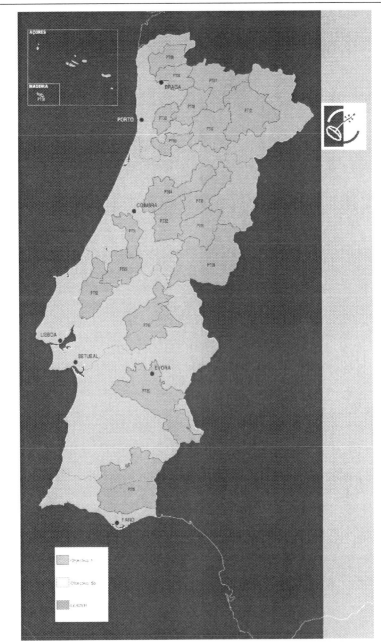

Figure 10.2   One of Europe's 217 Leader 1 Areas – PT 20
(Courtesy of the Leader Observatory, AEIDL, Brussels)

Figure 10.2 (continued)

ALENTEJO CENTRO

LEADER AREA	**Business Plan** (x 1000 ECU)
Objective: 1	Technical assistance **291**
Member State: Portugal	
Region: Alentejo	Vocational training **187**
District: Evora	
Type of area: Flat	Rural tourism **2713**
Surface area: 3592 km^2	
Population: 66,132 inhabitants	SMEs, handicraft, services **721**
Population density: 18 inhabitants/km^2	
Breakdown of the working population:	Developing agriculture produce **1545**
Agriculture 53%	
Industry 18%	Other purposes **111**
Services 29%	
Rate of unemployment: 15% (1992)	LAG's operation **497**
Demography:	
36% are less than 25 years old	
17% are more than 64 years old	**Total: 6065**

In the case of the Western Isles of Scotland, a strong emphasis was placed on working with and through local communities. A high proportion of LEADER staff time went into stimulating community involvement and action, with three field officers and a network of part-time locally based animateurs working to that end. An evaluation undertaken at the end of the programme commended both a shift in local attitudes away from a 'grant mentality' towards a more 'independent and self-thinking attitude', and more specifically a programme of community animation on the small islands of North and South Uist in the Outer Hebrides, which stimulated a number of innovative projects there.

Community participation and development was also a key theme of the South Pembrokeshire LEADER programme (Moseley & Cherrett, 1993). There, great weight was placed on encouraging each community to make its own appraisal of needs and opportunities and to draw up an 'action plan' which would be locally owned and to some extent locally delivered. The South Pembrokeshire programme evaluators concluded that from "interviews in the eleven communities

selected . . . a tremendous sense of approval and renewed motivation emerges in
. . . the considerable range of community activities which have been engendered
and the raised awareness and confidence which have been displayed . . . The
short time scale of funding has hindered the optimal initiation of a process requiring considerable sustained effort [but] this process . . . has been of substantial
benefit to significant numbers of people . . ."

Conclusion

The three case studies described above demonstrate the importance now attached
by several national and international agencies to the orchestration of co-ordinated
rural development programmes at the local level. In part this reflects an
acceptance that particular circumstances must be respected if wise investments
are to be made and value for money achieved. There is also an acknowledgement
that local people are a resource in their own right and that involving them as
partners not only serves to make use of their talents but also promises to develop
a pool of knowledge, expertise and enthusiasm which might well bear fruit
for years to come. In short, locally tailored rural development programmes are
an exercise in 'capacity building' and sustainability as much as anything else
(Chapter 3 has more to say on these points).

There is no blueprint to guide the designation of appropriate areas for this task.
Experience suggests that areas with fewer than 10 000 inhabitants are likely to lack
sufficient resources not least of local leadership, while those with over 100 000 inhabitants tend to exhibit a poor sense of cohesion and real 'manageability' when
it comes to promoting a bottom-up approach. More important than mere size,
however, is a sense of local identity and common destiny. This is where an area
such as the Forest of Dean, with a shared culture born of its coal-mining past and
its 'peninsular' location, sandwiched as it is between the rivers Wye and Severn,
has an advantage over, say, the vast Northumberland RDA stretching from the
outskirts of Tyneside to the Scottish border, or some of the extensive LEADER
areas in Wales and Scotland.

Be that as it may, the challenge of area-based rural development programming
for the rural community worker, or for the lay person concerned with the future
of his or her local community, is to get to grips with the complex and protracted
process of setting priorities across perhaps fifty such communities. The planners
will, or should, be at pains to foster only those projects which promise to give a
real spur to the dynamic of rural development. Mere 'bright ideas', unrelated to
the wider picture, are not what the exercise is supposed to be about, nor are they
likely to prove sustainable in the longer term.

Chapter 11

Rural Community Development: Looking Forward

Prediction and preference run parallel courses. Over time many commentators have sought to record either how life will be in the future or how it should be: from Plato's *Republic*, to Sir Thomas More's *Utopia*, written in 1516, and portraying a perfectly organized and happy island community. More recently writers like Samuel Butler described *Erewhon* ('nowhere', almost backwards) in 1872, and the polymath William Morris reported *News from Nowhere*, another visionary text, as a waking dream. Some country watchers have similarly charted a course specifically for rural areas; the agricultural economist, C.S. Orwin, writing in 1945, gave a vivid portrait of what might be. Some of it has come to pass, and in other respects he was way 'off-beam':

> Let us try to reconstruct the scene which might greet the eyes of another Rip van Winkle who had fallen asleep, say, in 1940 and awakened a generation later . . .

> The landscape . . . would show notable changes . . . The many awkward little fields . . . the overgrown hedgerows and choked ditches . . . all were gone. The trim hedges enclosed larger fields. There were no horses to be seen . . . everywhere there was the suggestion of technological changes, all of which seemed to promote a greater activity on the land.

> . . . Gone were the dilapidated old barns . . . in short the homestead impressed him, just as the fields had done, with its air of order and efficiency . . . He wondered at the number of young men he saw about the place and learned that this reconstructed homestead was the headquarters of a large farming enterprise, built up from an amalgamation of several smaller farms. Only through the larger unit had it been found possible . . . to give full scope to highly qualified management and to skilled workers . . .

> The isolated cottages in the fields, remote from neighbours, public services and the amenities of village life, seemed to have disappeared . . . Nearly all the men, it seemed, lived in houses in the villages, and came to their work on

motor bicycles. The farming, he found, was carried on much more intensively [and] caused a considerable demand for seasonal labour . . . he betook himself next to the village of his youth . . . the place had grown but not beyond recognition. New houses came out to meet him, pleasant houses, larger than those which he had known . . . the new houses merged almost imperceptibly into the old village without incongruity. . . Most of the new houses were occupied, it seemed, by workers in a factory which had been moved out of Birmingham and set up on a site about five miles away.

. . . the ugly Victorian Vicarage . . . had become the Community Centre – the focus of all the social activity in the village . . . served for the health clinic, county library, clubrooms, adult education classrooms, canteen and restaurant . . .

The school in which van Winkle had been educated . . . had gone . . . there was a new and larger general shop and a butcher's business where none had been before, but the same little post office still served . . . There was no suggestion about the place of a divided community, of an old village and a new housing estate. On the contrary, Rip van Winkle had an impression of a virile, well-knit society. . . There was a vigour and activity about the place . . .

The art of prediction must therefore be approached with humility and in the certain knowledge that inaccuracies are inevitable! Once more Rip van Winkle feels his eyes heavy lidded and in 1997 falls into the arms of Morpheus, but this time he experiences not one, but two dreams of life for the next generation. In the first the clouds darken . . .

A Future Malign
A uniformed security guard touches his cap, apparently recognizing van Winkle's familiar face. He is allowed through the perimeter fence which keeps out 'undesirables'. Rip van Winkle glances back at a scene of desolation: over-grown hedges, abandoned fields and, in one corner, a series of industrial-scale greenhouses for intensive cultivation. A small 'shanty town' catches the eye, where young adults live. They also seem to spill out from dilapidated farm buildings no longer required for agricultural use.

Inside, the village looks prosperous with the houses and well-tended enclosed gardens in good order. There is hardly any sound of activity, except for the muted drone of windmills supplying electricity to individual properties. Half the village lies shuttered, empty or with the curtains drawn: it only comes to life at weekends and most particularly in the short summer season. The remaining houses betray a flickering half-light: people are word-processing, using pictorial-telephones, faxing information, video-conferencing and ordering shopping and other goods for delivery, remote banking and undertaking multi-lingual translation by computer. In one sitting room a man struts about with an attached headset, recreating some virtual experience.

There is no village shop, post office, school, pub, general practitioner, dentist, chemist, public telephone box or bus service. The only facility is the Museum of Virtual Village Life ("step back in time to experience a village November 5th party from the year 1997"!). A sign is glowing in the window: 'museum and heritage artefact dispensary open June-August only'. There are few signs of local distinct-iveness; new houses display a uniformity of design, and the redundant parish church has been flattened to make way for luxury flats. The old school is now an antique shop. Satellite dishes, antennae and aerials adorn the skyline. But the village has undoubtedly grown in size and absorbed any run-down and derelict buildings.

There are few, if any, children in evidence, but plenty of people in early or advanced retirement. This is a very private lifestyle where a car remains essential for infrequent trips to centralized services like the family clinic, hospital and old people's facility, travelling for entertainment and visits to relatives. Petrol is a luxury, however, and as far as possible, the new technologies represent the life-line for villagers.

The village hall is now a residence; the village itself a 'detached suburb' where people co-exist, living and working in isolation from each other – a collection of individual lives with no apparent unifying or cohesive attachment. A regional authority and myriad non-elected quangos ensure safety on the highways, control of excessive pollution and exert control over other major issues of general importance. Most local councils have ceased to exist as households operate without recourse to common purpose. This is an exclusive, selfish, outwardly attractive but hollow village existence for employed, middle income, middle class couples in their middle years.

Future Benign
It is still early afternoon. Even before Rip van Winkle's eyes open he hears sounds of activity: children ragging and rushing in the school playground, the chime of the church bell, movement along the main street, people coming, going, passing, talking. His eyes are open now. Beyond the village are a number of young people digging, carrying, and tending the fields. Light machinery is in evidence, but this is an extensive agriculture employing people on the land and requiring fewer inputs of costly artificial fertilizers and pesticides.

Gone are the dilapidated old barns: they have become storage and headquarters for the village farm co-operative, selling organic and locally distinct produce. There is also new development in evidence, with a mix of younger and older residents working together to construct small, two or three bedroom, flats and houses for first-time buyers and retired members of the community. New houses stood before him, pleasant structures, some of traditional local materials while others were in glass, timber and even some semi-permanent 'benders' (tent-like structures) built in durable and colourful plastics.

Everywhere was alive with activity and change: the Victorian vicarage had become the Community Centre which was the focus of all the social activity in the village and served for the health clinic, county library and learning centre, tele-cottage, post (and E-mail) office, clubroom, adult education classrooms, canteen and restaurant. Some of these businesses generate income which has been recycled into environmental improvements and promotion of further training opportunities within the community.

The parish council was based here too, and a stream of enquirers came and went from their offices, seeking planning permission, consulting the part-time village development assistant, complaining about the late collection of household refuse. A background droning noise caught van Winkle's attention – the sound of a small windfarm (and tourist attraction) at the edge of the village. There was an additional community-heating plant using straw and household waste.

The community centre had a voice-sensitive information point by the entrance. On request it gave out details of local societies and contacts: the environmental action group; Workers Education Association classes in languages, computing, active citizenship; better-by-design – a forum that villagers with ideas for new local buildings could attend; parent and toddlers; day centre for older residents and their younger relatives; a local history and futures society; the 'twisty roads' group that arranges a communal Easter-egg hunt for the village children; fire-works night and harvest gatherings open to the entire population and using gifts of money, food and other practical assistance from villagers. The range of self-help and self-reliance was impressive.

A guide appears as a lay priest and offers a commentary on what has been seen so far: "The individual is rooted in the community where economic relationships are personal, and where a sense of corporate identity is fostered by the pattern of daily work; and yet the village is economically and culturally open, in constant communication with places and people beyond the parish. The modern lifestyle thus has a mixture of features from both the medieval and the industrial age, and yet is a radical development from both" (Weyer, 1986).

With a faint twinge of recognition, Rip van Winkle noticed a flickering half-light within some of the houses: the occupants are word-processing, using pictorial telephones, faxing information and ordering by computer major items for delivery. The Village Interactive Museum of the Past and Future, dedicated to Alexis de Tocqueville, allows you to take a 'walk' through the virtual village, making different choices and decisions as you go.

This appraisal of opinion by resident and visitor alike is logged, and a digest reported to the parish council on a monthly basis for discussion and potential action. One of the exhibits shows a grey and crackly reconstruction of a man, de Tocqueville, speaking about democracy in 1835: "The strength of free peoples resides in the local community. Local institutions are to liberty what primary schools are to science; they put it within the people's reach; they teach people to appreciate its peaceful enjoyment and accustom them to make use of it. Without local institutions a nation may give itself a free government but it has not got the spirit of liberty" (de Tocqueville, cited in Rendell & Ward, 1989).

The sleeper awakes in 1997 with much to ponder.

From Here to There
The second scenario, to be attainable, requires that villages are active, balanced and caring: **active** in the sense that people do not just live there but many work in the village as well, and work implies not simply a job but also a wider commitment to community life; **balanced** in terms of the village broadly mirroring the social structure of society as a whole where there are old and young, those on high and low incomes (and no income), those from a variety of ethnic and cultural backgrounds; **caring** with "a shared acceptance of responsibility beyond one's own garden gate. Responsibility for those without secure jobs, comfortable homes and good health – and for the community as a whole" (Moseley, 1993).

There are some recent signs of hope. In 1994 the European Council for the Village and Small Town (ECOVAST) published a Strategy for Rural Europe which sought "integrated action between different arms of government, and between government and local people. We expect the people to be consulted and involved." By 1995 the Scottish Office had committed itself to "partnerships, bringing together at local level all the agencies with responsibilities in rural areas, including the local council, community groups and private and voluntary interests." The English 'Rural White Paper' similarly pledged central government to work collaboratively "with local people rather than impose top-down solutions" (Hansard, 1995).

Table 11 Government and Community Development (1995): Summary of Commitments in the English 'Rural' White Paper (Cm 3016)

- A *Cabinet Committee* to co-ordinate and review central government rural policy.

- *Partnerships* between relevant quangos, and at a local level via non-statutory Rural Strategies.

- A definite steer towards *self-help*, building on existing rural voluntary action.

- A commitment to *subsidiarity:* opportunities for parish and town councils to take on new duties (to be paid for by higher local taxation) devolved by principal authorities.

- Agreement to review local authority costs of delivering rural services (the *'sparsity factor'*).

- Retention and encouragement of *distinctive and living communities.*

- Measures to ensure that people "have a reasonable prospect of finding *affordable housing . . ."* ·

- Measures to facilitate *access* to a range of services such as village shops and schools.

- Support for the Rural Development Commission, *Rural Community Councils* and their transport and housing 'brokers/enablers'.

- Acknowledgement of the value of *community-managed* buses, needs surveys, appraisals and design statements.

Source: Clark, 1995

The next step is to put into operation such broad indications of backing so that "local, national and global policies understand and support the role of local communities, and shape public services and economic systems accordingly. We need policies which strengthen the ability of the people, especially those in disadvantaged situations, to control their own local economic and social conditions . . ." (Chanan, 1995).

"Self help and independence are traditional strengths of rural communities. People in the countryside have always needed to take responsibility for looking after themselves and each other. They do not expect government to solve all their problems for them and they know that it is they who are generally best placed to identify their own needs and the solutions to them.

In any case local decision making is likely to be more responsive to local circumstances than universal plans. Improving the quality of life in the country-side starts with local people and local initiative." (DoE & MAFF, 1995)

It is the interpretation and style of implementation of the sentiments outlined in the above quote that will, in the immediate future, influence the degree to which rural community development and community action lead toward a broadly malign or benign outcome. At the sceptical end of the spectrum the Bishop of Southwark, for example, has commented on the White Paper's "fundamentally important and excellent policy objectives. But the brutal truth is that most of them cost money and require political will to make available resources through the tax system to support objectives which are widely endorsed by the public at large. If our political culture slides back into the simplistic mindset that spending public money is bad ... most of the White Paper will be a dead duck" (Hansard, 1995). And the Government has committed no extra finance to implement the 'rural' White Paper: "The White Paper has been described as the longest unpriced menu in the world" (Lord Beaumont in Hansard, 1995).

As long ago as the 1920s there were official calls to "put resources at the call of local needs, intermediaries are indispensable, and for every reason co-operation must be sought with the many people and agencies already at work in the country, some of whom have long and valuable experience" (Rural Industries Intelligence Bureau, undated – c.1925). Therefore a generalized commitment from government and other agencies must not become a convenient peg on which to hang the wholesale withdrawal of the state, at national and local level, or the private sector from the countryside. Voluntary action and self-help are obviously essential and appropriate means by which to involve and service rural communities, but this should complement and extend public provision and not replace it. Government should seize this "opportunity to enhance community participation by increased support for development of community groups and infrastructure ... Much of the funding for community development is project based and short-term. It should be seen as a core activity within an on-going funding regime" (ACRE, 1996).

A Swedish commentator, Bengt Dahlgren (1995) argues, that a shorter paid working week and working lifespan could prove highly beneficial in fostering dynamic local communities: "If we had more time, this would create the conditions for large-scale local development work ... It would perhaps mean the emergence of a kind of private-social enterprise (community projects run as social co-operatives) in a third sector" – that is, telecottages, community-run shops, credit unions and other community businesses.

There also remain doubts about the ability of community-grounded action to do more than 'tidy the chairs on board the Titanic'. The 'process and the product' may be construed as no more than 'window dressing', to distract attention from more fundamental questions of equity, distribution of resources and opportunity within society. As Malcolm Moseley (1985) observed in relation to the efficacy of 'patchworkers' and by extension rural community development itself: ". . . whether a 'rural catalyst' could ever help the rural disadvantaged to 'take on the system' remains unproven . . . What he or she can do is to help rural people to help one another and thereby to make life marginally more agreeable. A not unworthy objective". But Dahlgren (1995) construes this in a positive light, pointing to the fact that it is "in the nature of creation that the new is often small. Thus there has to be a great deal of it. There must be [an acceptance of] a multiplicity of ideas and initiatives. Nor, when we evaluate the results and effects, must we expect rapid and major results". The coalescing of many individual projects may indeed reach a critical mass that brings community development from the margins to the centre of decision-making and implementation. Furthermore, Elisabeth Skinner (in Chapter 6) points to communal activity as "a strong element of late twentieth century middle-class culture": this may provide the launchpad for considerable future community-based activity; but only if there are real opportunities for new and disadvantaged people within a community to have access to and influence on the form of that process.

A further positive facet working in favour of 'community development', arises from its status in folk-memory and an almost universal perception that it is 'a good thing'. Politically, community development occupies a convenient neutral space between left and right: with socialists striving for a re-creation of unity and communal concern – during 1995 Tony Blair proclaimed that the "idea of rural communities has always been far stronger in Labour thinking than people make out . . . one of the great things about rural life is that there is a deep sense of community" (*Daily Telegraph*, 22 September). The Liberal Democrats on the other hand celebrate the power and desirability of locally-based action, while the Conservatives seek to promote individual opportunity and responsibility and limited state intervention: their policies have already been discussed in relation to the 1995 rural white paper.

Other positive indicators of increasing rural development based on community approaches include moves to delegate powers to parish and town councils, 'charters' covering the delivery of various local government functions and a recognition that sustainability in practice requires local consent and dynamism.

Rural community workers have a number of trends running in their favour:

Repopulation of the countryside potentially constitutes something of a transfusion – in the form of new blood, new ideas and fresh enthusiasm for locally-based action. Sheepscombe village (Gloucestershire) highlights the possibilities for commuters as activists.

Telework could provide a new economic *raison d'être* for the countryside. Social health and welfare must spring from economic vitality and sustainability. There can be no permanent state 'crutch' to prop up rural settlements.

There is now a considerable weight of experience in joint working and ***partnership***, at an organizational, programme, policy and project level: the DoE & MAFF publication of a joint 'Rural White Paper' in 1995; the Cabinet Environment Committee adopting a broad rural remit; RDC, Countryside Commission and English Nature collaborations to promote County Rural Strategies; and Rural Action for the Environment. English Rural Development Programmes, EU LEADER and Objective 5b, and Civic Trust regeneration schemes, are other examples of collective action founded on the participation of local communities. A recent report on 'Community Involvement in Estate Regeneration Partnerships' (McArthur *et al.*, 1996) sets down five key aspects of good practice for community organizations wishing to maximize their effect on regeneration programmes, "and for other agencies committed to ensuring meaningful community involvement":

1. *Capacity building:* a protracted period of community development, lasting perhaps five years, "seems to be required before a community has the confidence to become involved in a comprehensive regeneration partnership".

2. *Engaging the community:* dialogue and publicity regarding the early development of a top-down initiative "can engage local interest and help develop a sense of ownership over the regeneration process".

3. *Organising for partnership:* "Community-based umbrella organisations assist in involving a wide range of local interests and present a single point of contact for both local residents and other partners". A community should have use of the same type and level of resources that other partners enjoy. Objectives and realistic time-scales need to be agreed by all parties at the outset. "Structures and processes should be kept as simple and informal as possible".

4. *Heightening the impact of community contributions:* development of accountable community organizations can strengthen dealings with other, external, partner agencies. Communities must find ways of articulating their views in 'behind the scenes' meetings that inevitably form part of the regeneration process.

5. *The afterlife:* regeneration stands a better chance of continuation if "the community is left in charge, perhaps of key assets, after the end of the formal initiative. This, however, requires resources and a commitment to build up the capacity of the community during the regeneration process."

Many partnerships make use of animateurs, *catalysts* or community development workers; based with Rural Community Councils, the Civic Trust, RDPs, or Local Authorities. Direct action by these individuals, and over time as these people gain promotion to positions of increased power with regard to policy making and budgetary control, can reinforce the mainstream status of community development.

There is also greater *sophistication* of voluntary sector activity in the form of agency work of various kinds, such as community care contracts with local authority Social Services departments, development of affordable housing through RCCs and housing associations.

Rural *Voluntarism* is widespread and officially sanctioned by government in relation to community-run buses, village appraisals, parental involvement in schools, neighbourhood and 'farm watch' schemes, Rural Action for the Environment, lay preachers, retained fire-fighters, and the enlistment of special constables. Significant voluntary action is also fostered by organizations like Community Service Volunteers, with around 30 000 unpaid helpers undertaking work each year across England and Wales. Look too at the tremendous growth of interest in pressure groups such as the Royal Society for the Protection of Birds (RSPB), whose membership rocketed from 98 000 to 852 000 between 1971-91, or Friends of the Earth which, over the same period, went from 1000 to 111 000 members (Warburton, 1994). The Volunteer Centre UK estimated that 23 million adults are involved in volunteering each year (1991 figure).

Subsidiarity: decision-making at the lowest, appropriate, level. Local government reorganization across England, Wales and Scotland is already producing new forms of service agreement and delegation of powers involving principal authorities and parish councils. For example, since 1993 Taunton Deane Borough Council (Somerset) has piloted the devolution of some planning controls "closer to the local community... empowering each participating parish council to deal with a range of planning applications within its area" (Taunton Deane Borough Council, 1995). Such moves are supported in the 1995 English Rural White Paper.

Sustainability as a concept, and in reality, demands parochial determination of local priorities and action; additionally there must be "a new vision of what a genuinely sustainable society would be like, emphasising the maximum level of regional and subregional self-sufficiency and social cohesion" (Chanan, 1995).

The new town of Bamberton, British Columbia, with a projected population of 12 000 people, for example, may offer a glimpse of how, in practice, 'eco-community design' might look: the aim is to develop on the site of a massive former cement works, on Vancouver Island. 200 000 trade union members have invested their pension funds in the 20-year completion of this project. There is a conscious attempt to "design sustainability into almost every aspect of the future community's life": sewage treatment to produce compost for re-use on the land; a full range of facilities to cut commuting by 60 per cent; links with local producers "to provide them with a stable market and residents with a regular supply of locally grown organic food" (Dauncey, 1993). In pursuit of "a strong sense of community and a high quality of life, in a prosperous post-industrial economy... ecologically sustainable lifestyles in harmony with the natural world", all parties have signed up to the Bamberton Code.

THE BAMBERTON CODE

We, the builders and residents of the town of Bamberton, stand by the following intentions:

1. **That Bamberton represents** a way of living which seeks to serve the needs both of our own generation, and of generations to come.
2. **That Bamberton represents** a new possibility for the way people co-exist with nature, upholding the ideal of resonsible stewardship, and seeking to be ecologically sustainable in the use of natural resources such as water, soil, habitat, energy and raw materials.
3. **That Bamberton represents** a rediscovery of the traditional virtues of community, being conducive to social interaction, care and mutual support, encouraging of responsibility in the pursuit of shared goals, and supportive of cultural and artistic richness.
4. **That Bamberton represents** a new possibility for the building of a self-reliant, local community economy, emphasizing enterprise and initiative; the contribution of labor; mutual economic support; innovation, research and development; personal, social and global responsibility; and long-term ecological sustainability.
5. **That Bamberton represents** a positive opportunity for all who call Bamberton home, being encouraging of creativity, learning and growth, and nurturing of a deep appreciation of the gift of life.

The Code and the Design Principles will be used to guide future development, and to keep future partners, builders and residents mindful of the intentions and commitments underlying the project.

Once built, a town may exist for thousands of years. Perhaps more than anyone else, the builders and designers of a new town are accountable to future generations, and their unspoken needs. In honour of this trust, they must endeavour to reflect the needs of the future in the designs of the present.

Figure 11.1

There is new and significant *money* to fuel community-based ideas, in the form of National Lottery and Millennium funding.

Most of the above could, however, prove negative in their effects on community development. In particular repopulation may continue to polarize rural communities; telework might inflict yet more insecure and poorly paid work on isolated areas; voluntary action could induce underfunding and state withdrawal from the countryside; sustainability might be used as an excuse to do nothing for the rural economy. To make rural development a reality, therefore, becomes a case of 'seizing the opportunities'.

Take Your Partners

Determining Partnerships and Funding Packages

Spend fifteen minutes trying to match agencies to the project under consideration; you should aim to justify your selections! Who do you consider can help and why, in terms of money, advice etc.? You may need to make certain assumptions – do this, but make explicit to yourself what these are. A suggested, although not definitive, listing is given at the end of this Section.

The hypothetical projects:

1. *A Redundant building with the potential for tourism use.*

2. *A Telecottage based in local church (C of E) school: community-based economic and social development project utilising information technology.*

3. *Village Shop-cum-Post Office threatened with closure: potential community-run alternative.*

And the hypothetical range of assistance:

> Rural Development Commission (RDC)
> British Telecom
> Business in the Community (BiC)
> Local Education Authority
> Parish Council
> Diocesan Education Board
> District Council Economic Development Officer
> District Council Development Control and Local Plan Officers
> County Council Economic Development Officer
> Countryside Commission
> English Heritage
> Regional Tourist Board
> Training and Enterprise Council (TEC/LEC – Scotland)
> National Association for Small Schools (NASS)

The Telecottage Association
Community: share ownership in business
Post Office Counters
County Council Co-operatives Development Officer
Action with Communities in Rural England.
Private sector businesses
European Union funding
Grant-making Trusts
Rural Community Council Field Officer
RDC Shops Adviser
District Council Rates Department
Royal Institute of British Architects – Community Building grant
District Council Tourism Officer

In addition see how many of these agencies you can correctly place according to the sector to which they belong (e.g. Countryside Commission – part of the private sector?!).

Suggested answers:

1. A Redundant building with the potential for tourism use

Rural Development Commission (RDC) – a quango offering grants and advice to promote socio-economic development in rural England. Specifically redundant buildings grants and relevant advice.

District Council Economic Development Officer – potential grant aid; advice on available work space.

District Council Development Control and Local Plan Officers – 'statutory smoothing' in terms of gaining planning permission.

County Council Economic Development Officer – potential grant aid; advice on available work space.

Countryside Commission – a quango funding and advising on developments which encourage protection of landscape and public enjoyment of the same.

English Heritage – a quango funding and advising on developments which protect historic properties and encourage public enjoyment of these.

Regional Tourist Board – marketing advice, contacts and statistical information on local tourist trade.

Private sector businesses – possible paying customers utilising new centre for product launches, corporate hospitality etc.

Parish Council – small-scale finance and support for planning permissions etc.

European Union funding – in vulnerable rural areas and supporting diversification of the rural economy (e.g. under Objectives 5b, 2 or the Leader II programme).

Royal Institute of British Architects – Community Building grant; specialist advice on building conversion.

District Council Tourism Officer – publicity, possible grant aid; leverage with other departments or agencies.

2. A Telecottage based in a local church (C of E) school: community-based economic and social development project utilizing information technology

British Telecom – philanthropy based on self-interest; possible grant assistance or help-in-kind.

Business in the Community (BiC) – potential funding, help-in-kind, and contacts with influential (national and regionally-based) companies.

Local Education Authority – 'statutory smoothing', possible financial and officer assistance (e.g. community tutors).

Parish Council – small-scale finance and support for planning permissions etc.

District Council Economic Development Officer – potential financial help; advice on available work space plus clients.

Diocesan Education Board – sanction the use of church-owned property; possible financial help.

Training and Enterprise Council (TEC) – grant aid for training and job creating projects.

County Economic Development team – potential financial assistance and advice on available work space. Leverage with other departments, for example, County Education Service.

RDC – a quango offering grants and advice to promote socio-economic development in rural England. Specifically, finance to create new rural jobs and innovation.

Potential EU funding – for vulnerable rural areas and supporting diversification of the rural economy.

National Association for Small Schools (NASS) – contacts and good practice networking.

The Telecottage Association – contacts and good practice networking; possible entree to funding.

Grant-making Trusts – money for community-based schemes.

3. Village Shop-cum-Post Office threatened with closure: potential community-run alternative

Rural Community Council Field Officer – advice on charitable status; contacts and good practice information; possible 'seed-corn' grant to start-up.

RDC Shops Adviser – specialist, practical advice on trading effectively; possible RDC finance.

.ict Council Rates Department – potential business rate exemption or reduction.

District Council Economic Development Section – potential financial assistance and advice on available work space plus clients.

Parish Council – small-scale finance and support for planning permissions etc.

Community: share ownership in business – secure base on which to found community business.

Post Office Counters – potential finance; help incorporate sub-post office as part of the shop. Publicity.

County Co-operatives Development Officer – specialist advice; leverage in and outside the authority.

Action with Communities in Rural England – dissemination of good practice, plus useful contacts.

Acronyms

ACC	Association of County Councils
ACoRA	Archbishops' Commission on Rural Areas
ACRE	Action with Communities in Rural England
ADC	Association of District Councils
AONB	Area of Outstanding Natural Beauty
BiC	Business in the Community
BTCV	British Trust for Conservation Volunteers
CCN	Community Council of Northumberland
CDF	Community Development Foundation
CLA	County Landowners Association
CLOC	Community Learning Opportunities Centre
CofE	Church of England
CoSIRA	Council for Small Industries in Rural Areas
CPRE	Council for the Protection of Rural England
CROP	Church Reaching Out to People
CVS	Council of Voluntary Service
DfEE	Department for Education and Employment
DoE	Department of the Environment
ECOVAST	European Council for the Village and Small Town
EH	English Heritage
GM	Grant Maintained
IMP	Integrated Mediterranean Programme
IRD	Integrated Rural Development programme
LEADER	Liaison Entre Actions de Développement de l'Economie Rurale

LGMB	Local Government Management Board
LMS	Local accountability for Management of Schools
MAFF	Ministry of Agriculture, Fisheries and Food
MEP	Member of the European Parliament
MoD	Ministry of Defence
NALC	National Association of Local Councils
NASS	National Association for Small Schools
NCC	Nature Conservancy Council
NCVO	National Council for Voluntary Organizations
NFU	National Farmers' Union
NFWI	National Federation of Women's Institutes
NIMBY	Not In My Back Yard
NGO	Non-Governmental Organization
NP	National Park
NT	National Trust
NWR	National Women's Register
PCC	Parochial Church Council
PTA	Parent Teacher Association
RCC	Rural Community Council
RDA	Rural Development Area
RDC	Rural Development Commission
RDP	Rural Development Programme
RSNC	Royal Society for Nature Conservation
RSPB	Royal Society for the Protection of Birds
RSPCA	Royal Society for the Prevention of Cruelty to Animals
RTPI	Royal Town Planning Institute
RV	Rural Voice
TEC	Training and Enterprise Council
WEA	Workers Educational Association
WI	Women's Institute
YFC	Young Farmers' Clubs

Bibliography

ACRE, *Village Halls in England*, ACRE, 1988.

ACRE, Rural Adult Education Project, Doing by Learning, ACRE, 1989.

ACRE, Policy Paper, Inquiry into the Rural White Paper: ACRE's Terms of Reference, ACRE, 1996.

Allenheads Residents Action Committee, Allenheads Village Appraisal: The Way Ahead, May 1986.

Allenheads Trust, Allenheads: Second Village Appraisal, 1992.

Archbishops' Commission on Rural Areas, *Faith in the Countryside*, Churchman Press, 1990.

Association of County Councils, *Consent Upon a Sure Foundation*, 1992.

Association of District Councils, *Closer to the People*, 1990.

Bailey, R., *The Crisis of the Rural School*, SPCK, 1955.

Baker Associates, *Directions for Local Agenda 21 – Action for Local Environmental Change*, Countryside Commission, English Heritage and English Nature, 1996.

Ball, A., *Modern Politics and Government*, Macmillan, 1988.

Barnes, L., *At the Grassroots – Developing Rural Work: Notes from Development Workers in Rural Areas*, NCVO (Rural Team), 1994a.

Barnes, L., *Reaching Out to Rural Communities: Tools for Developing Rural Work*, NCVO (Rural Team), 1994b.

Barakonyi, K., Role of the German 'face' in the Existence of a Village Local Government, Pollack Mihaly Technical College (Hungary), 1995.

BBC Television (BBC1), The Lowdown, 21 August 1995.

Bell, A. & Sigsworth, A., *The Heart of the Community*, Mousehold Press, 1992.

Bishop, J., (BDOR Ltd), *Community Action – an Appraisal*, Countryside Commission, 1991.

Bovaird, T., Green, J., Martin, S., Millward, A. & Tricker M., *Evaluation of Rural Action for the Environment: Three Year Review of Efficiency and Effectiveness*. Public Sector Management Research Centre, Aston University, 1995

Brown, P., Public gets vote on which buildings are worth saving, *The Guardian*, 9 March 1995.

Buller, H. & Wright, S., *Rural Development: Problems and Practices*, Avebury, 1990.

Burnet, J., Cumbria Case Study, the implementation experience, *Countynews*, July/August 1995.

Champion, A., Marching across England's green and pleasant land: the progress of counterurbanisation, Department of Geography, University of Newcastle-upon-Tyne, 1991.

Chanan, G., Implications for Local Practice, in *Out of the Shadows*, European Foundation for the Improvement of Living and Working Conditions, 1992; reproduced in UK by Community Development Foundation, 1994.

Chanan, G., Sustainable Communities: an International Perspective, paper to Developing the Rural Economy Conference, 19-20 October 1995, ICOM, ACRE, CWS, NCVO, CORT and RDC.

Citizen's Charter Unit, *Rural Services Checklist*, 1995.

Clark, D., Country Patch: Some local rural development projects, *Rural Voice*, 1985.

Clark, D., *Community Action in the Countryside: a review of RCC roles in conservation, recreation and access issues*, ACRE, 1989a.

Clark, D., *Practical Partnership, Districts Working with Rural Community Councils: A Good Practice Guide*, ACRE/Association of District Councils, 1989b.

Clark, D., The Diversity of Local Government Structures within Great Britain, Cheltenham and Gloucester College of Higher Education, March 1995a.

Clark, D., Local Councils as Partners: A new role for Parish and Town Councils, presentation to In Partnership Summer School, Cheltenham and Gloucester College of Higher Education, 1995b.

Clark, D., Rural White Paper 1995, a guide for RCCs, ACRE Rural Briefing, December 1995c.

Clarke, L., *The Chymical Wedding*, Jonathan Cape, 1989.

Clifford, S. & King, A., *Holding Your Ground*. Temple Smith, 1985.

Clifford, S. & King, A., *Celebrating Local Distinctiveness*, Common Ground, for Rural Action, 1994.

Cloke, P., in *Writing the Rural: five cultural geographies*, Paul Chapman Publishing, 1994.

Cloke, P., Thomas, C. & Milbourne, P., *Lifestyles in Rural England*, Rural Development Commission, 1994.

Committee for Rural Hampshire, *Annual Report*, 1992.

Community Council of Devon, *Community Economic Development in Devon*, 1994.

Community Council of Northumberland, *Village Schools and their Community*, 1994.

Community Development Foundation (CDF), *Annual Review*, 1994/95.

Conroy, C. & Litvinoff, M., Sustainable Development, in *The Green Reader*, ed. Dobson, A, André Deutsch, 1991.

Copeland Borough Council, Cumbria Association of Local Councils and Cumbria County Council, *A Code of Practice*, 1995.

Council of Europe, Committee on Agriculture and Rural Development, European Rural Charter (First Draft), 14 September 1994.

Countryside Commission, *Corporate Strategy, 1989-90*, 1989.

Countryside Commission, *Sustainability and the English Countryside*, 1993.

Countryside Commission, English Nature and English Heritage, *Ideas into Action for Local Agenda 21*, 1996.

Countryside Commission, English Nature and the Rural Development Commission, *Rural Action for the environment – An Introduction*, 1992a.

Countryside Commission, English Nature and the Rural Development Commission, *Rural Strategies*, 1992b.

Countryside and Community Research Unit, ACRE and Gloucestershire Rural Community Council, *Village Appraisals; Helping you Plan for your community's future*, Cheltenham and Gloucester College of Higher Education, 1991.

Coxall, B. & Robins, L., *Contemporary British Politics* (2nd edition), Macmillan, 1994.

Crutcher, M. & Scott, D., *Rural Realities: A Training Guide for Community Groups and Professional Workers*, Community Education Development Centre/Peak District Rural Deprivation Forum and the University of Manchester School of Social Policy, 1995.

Cumbria County Council, *Neighbourhood Forums Information*, Neighbourhood Services Section, 1995.

Dahlgren, B., Some Reflections on the Periphery, US–Swedish Seminar on Development in Marginal Areas, Karlstad, 1989.

Dahlgren, B., On Development at Large and in Small Places – an Extended Summary, Karlstad, 1995.

Daily Telegraph, Blair Woos Country Sports Lobby, 22nd September 1995.

Dauncey, G., Eco-Community Design, *In Context*, 35, 1993.

Department of the Environment, *Development Plans and Regional Planning Guidance*, PPG12, HMSO, 1992.

Department of the Environment, *UK Biodiversity Action Plan*, 1995a.

Department of the Environment, Decisions on Parishes Announced, DoE News Release, 11th July 1995b.

Department of the Environment, *Involving Communities in Urban and Rural Regeneration,: A Guide for Practitioners*, Regeneration Research Summary, 46, 1995c.

Department of the Environment and Ministry of Agriculture, Fisheries and Food, *Rural England: A Nation Committed To A Living Countryside*, Cm 3016, HMSO, 1995.

Derbyshire, H., *Not in Norfolk: Tackling the Invisibility of Racism*, Norfolk and Norwich Racial Equality Council, 1994.

Derounian, J.G., *Read All About it – starting or improving a newsletter*, Community Council of Devon, 1985.

Derounian, J.G., Money for Mining Areas Lies Idle, *Rural Viewpoint*, 48, April 1992a.

Derounian, J.G. (ed.), *The Village Strikes Back: breathing new life into rural communities*, Northern Network of Rural Development Programmes, 1992b.

Derounian, J.G., *Old Age Benefits: A Review of Rural Development Commission/ Help the Aged Joint Working*, RDC 1993a.

Derounian, J.G., *Rural Community Development in Jamtland, Central Sweden*, Northumberland Rural Development Programme, 1993b.

Derounian, J.G., *Another Country*, NCVO Publications, 1993c.

Derounian, J.G. & Moseley M.J., Rural Development in practice: the Northumberland Rural Development Programme process, *Town Planning Review* 65.4 (1994), 463–470.

Derrida, J., in Kearney, R. (ed.), *Dialogues with contemporary Continental thinkers*, Manchester University Press, 1984.

Dickens, C., *Hard Times*, Penguin edition, 1969.

Dower, M., Problems in application of EEC policies for rural development, CEPFAR European Conference, May 1991.

Dower, M., Rural Well-being in Europe, Cheltenham and Gloucester College of Higher Education lecture, April 1995.

Drucker, P.F., *Managing for the future*, Butterworth-Heinemann, 1992.

Duncan, G., Belonging in Etchington: An Interpretive Study of an East Sussex Village, University of Sussex, 1992.

Eames, C., Organisation and Adult Education in the North Derbyshire Coalfield, in Henderson, P. and Francis, D. (eds.), *Rural Action*, Pluto Press, 1993.

Eden District Council, Fellside and Moor: Report of the East Fellside and Alston Moor Project, 1986.

Ellwood, S., Nutley, S., Tricker, M. & Waterston, P., *Parish and Town Councils in England: A Survey*, HMSO, 1992.

English Heritage, *Annual Report and Accounts 1993/94*, 1994.

English Nature, *Sustainability in Practice*, English Nature, 1994.

European Council for the Village and Small Town (ECOVAST), *A Strategy for Rural Europe*, 1994.

Everitt, A., Time to Pump up Parish Politics, *Country Life*, 31 August 1995.

Fitzduff, N., Protest, Affirmation and Adult Education on the Loughshore, in Henderson, P. & Francis, D. (eds.), *Rural Action*, Pluto Press, 1993.

Fitzpatrick, A., Promoting our School, 1995a.

Fitzpatrick, A., Toddington County Primary School, Gloucestershire, a graphic presentation, 1995b.

Forest of Dean Rural Development Programme Committee, *Forest of Dean Rural Development Programme: a strategy 1995–2000*, 1995.

Francis, D. & Henderson, P., *Working with Rural Communities*, Macmillan, 1992.

Fulford, F., Dancing to the Quangos' Tune, *The Field*, July 1995.

Gilchrist, A., Community Development and Networking, Standing Conference of Community Development/Community Development Foundation, 1995.

Gillett, H., This Question of Politics, Letter to the Editor, *Local Council Review*, May 1995.

Graham, S., Best Practice in Developing Community Teleservice Centres, University of Manchester (CASR) and the University of Newcastle-upon-Tyne, Department of Town and Country Planning, 1992.

Grampian Regional Council, *Environmental Charter*, 1990.

Greeves, T. & Taylor, R.E., *The Local Jigsaw* (Information Pack for ACRE & Common Ground), 1987.

Gummer, J., quoted in Department of the Environment/MAFF joint News Release, Government Announces Rural White Paper, 12th October 1994.

Halliday, J., *Migration in Devon*, Devon County Council/University of Exeter, Department of Geography, 1991.

Hampshire County Council/Committee for Rural Hampshire, *Hampshire Rural Development Strategy*, 1991.

Hansard (House of Lords), Rural Areas: Integrated Policy, 463 (83), Proceedings on 30th April 1985.

Hansard (House of Lords), The Countryside, Proceedings on 7th November 1995.

Harper, S., The British Rural Community: An Overview of Perspectives, *Journal of Rural Studies*, 5, (2), 1989.

Hawtin, M., Hughes, G. & Percy-Smith, J., *Community Profiling (auditing social needs)*, Open University Press, 1994.

Henderson, P. & Francis, D. (eds.), *Rural Action*, Pluto Press, 1993.

Hoggart, K. & Buller, H., *Rural Development: A Geographical Perspective*, Croom Helm, 1987.

Hughes, E., Jigso; five years of community action, Past achievements and future developments, Rural Survey Research Unit, University of Wales, 1993.

International Union for the Conservation of Nature, Worldwide Fund for Nature and the United Nations' Environment Programme, *Caring for the Earth*, Earthscan, 1991.

Jack, I., In pursuit of Englishness, *Independent on Sunday*, 9 July 1995.

Jenner, C., 'It's Almost a Full Time Job', Letter to the Editor, *Local Council Review*, May 1995.

Kingston, P., An everyday story of hate, loathing, and country folk, *The Guardian (Society)*, 12 July 1995.

Kolek, C.R., *Elderly People in Eden – Independence and the Supportive Network*, Age Concern (Eden), 1993.

Kudian, M. (ed.), *Three Apples Fell From Heaven*, Hart-Davis, 1969.

Lawton, A. & Rose, A., *Organisation and Management in the Public Sector*, Pitman, 1991.

Lewis, C. Day, Watching Post, reproduced in *Modern Poetry*, Oxford University Press, 1971.

Lloyd, N., 'Small Schools in Rural Areas', ACRE Issue, 1995.

Local Government Management Board (LGMB), *Sustainable Development in Rural Areas*, 1994a.

Local Government Management Board, *Community Participation in Local Agenda 21*, 1994b.

Lumb, R., *Village Schools in Northumberland*, Community Council of Northumberland, 1983.

Mabey, R., in preface of Mabey, R., Clifford, S. & King, A., (eds), *Second Nature*, 1984.

McArthur, A., McGregor, A. & Hastings, A., quoted in 'Community involvement in estate regeneration partnerships', Joseph Rowntree Foundation, *Housing Research Findings*, 167, February 1996.

McCormick, J., *British Politics and the Environment*, Earthscan, 1991.

Milbourne, P., Rural Communities, Module pack on *Contemporary Rural Issues*, Department of Countryside and Landscape, Cheltenham and Gloucester College of Higher Education, 1995.

MINTEL International Group, *Regional Lifestyles*, 1992.

More, Sir T., *Utopia*, Penguin Classics edition, 1965.

Morrison, M., Whither now for Stirling's Albion?, *Planning Week*, 5 October 1995.

Moseley, M.J., The Waveney Project: The Role of the Catalyst in Rural Community Development, University of East Anglia, 1985.

Moseley, M.J., Rural Communities: The Challenge Ahead, Speech at ACRE Seminar, St. James's Palace, 23 March 1993.

Moseley M.J., Baseline Studies for local Rural Development Programmes: towards a methodology, Planning Practice and Research, 1996a.

Moseley M.J., The LEADER programme 1992-94: an assessment of a European area-based rural development programme, Unpublished: CCRU, Cheltenham & Gloucester College of Higher Education, 1996b.

Moseley, M.J., Parish Appraisals as a Tool of Rural Community Development: A review of the British experience, *Planning Practice and Research*, (in press).

Moseley, M.J. & Cherrett, T., Involving People in Local Development, LEADER Co-ordinating Unit/AEIDL, 1993.

Moseley, M.J., Derounian, J.G. & Allies, P., Parish Appraisals – a Spur to Local Action? A Review of the Gloucestershire and Oxfordshire Experience, *Town Planning Review*, July 1996.

Mulgan, G., Charity begins with home truths, *The Independent*, 20 July 1995.

National Association for the Support of Small Schools, News leak from Wales, *NASSSNEWS*, June 1995.

National Trust, *Countryside Matters: The National Trust at work in England, Wales and Northern Ireland*, 1992.

National Women Register, The aims of NWR, *The Register*, July 1995.

NCVO (National Council for Voluntary Organisations), *Voluntary Organisations Environmental Action Network: Contacts directory*, 1995.

NCVO (Rural Team), *Rural England – the Rural White Paper*, 1996.

Network News, Rural Development Council Changes Priority, *Network News*, Summer 1995.

Newby, H., *Green and Pleasant Land?* (2nd edition) Wildwood House, 1985.

Northumberland County Council (National Park Division), Northumberland National Park, Video, 1993.

Orwin, C.S., *Problems of the Countryside*, Cambridge University Press, 1945.

Orwell, G., *Animal Farm*, Penguin edition, 1945.

Packer, N., 2020 Vision, *Planning Week*, 15 June 1995.

Pahl, R., *Whose City? And other essays on sociology and planning*, Longman, 1970.

Parsons, M. (ed.), *Your Place or Mine: A review of how and why communities are looking after their local countryside*, RSNC (the Wildlife Trusts Partnership), 1992.

Peak National Park, *Two Villages Two Valleys*, 1990.

Phillips, D. & Karn, V.A., Race and Housing in a Property-owning Democracy, *New Community*, 18 (3), 1992.

Planning Week, The Ramblers' Association (Stop Press), 20 July 1995.

Puketapu-Hetet, E, *Maori Weaving*, Pitman, Auckland, 1989.

RDC, ICOM, CORT, ACRE and CWS, Developing the Rural Economy Conference, 19-20 October 1995.

Rendell, R. & Ward, C., *Undermining the Central Line*, Chatto Counter Blast, No. 7, 1989.

Reynolds, H. & Talbot, J., Capacity Building in Rural Communities, Workshop paper to ACRE Rural Life Conference, Community Council of Devon, 1995.

Rogers, A.W., Voluntarism, Self-help and Rural Community Development: Some Current Approaches, *Journal of Rural Studies* (3) 4, 1987.

Roome, N., Green Perspectives on Community and Public Policy, in Butcher, H., Glen, A., Henderson, P. & Smith, J., (eds.), *Community and Public Policy*, 1992.

Rowntree, J., quoted in *Search* 101 Joseph Rowntree Foundation, Spring 1995.

RTPI, *Rural white paper*, submission of representations to the DoE and the MAFF for consideration in the preparation of the proposed white paper, January 1995.

Rural Action National Development Team, Newsletters (first four issues 1992–1995).

Rural Development Commission, *Rural Development Areas 1994*, Policy Information, 1993a

Rural Development Commission, *The Future of the Rural Development Programme Process*, 1993b.

The Rural Development Commission, *1993/94 Annual Report*, 1994.

Rural Development Commission, Father Joe Long – Part of the Union, article in *Ruralfocus*, Winter 1994/95.

Rural Industries Intelligence Bureau, Village Life and Country Industries, Leaflet number 1, undated (circa 1925?).

Rural Voice Health Group, *Health Care in Rural England*, ACRE, 1992.

Rural Voice, *A Rural Strategy*, 1987.

Rural Voice, *Employment on the land: a new perspective*, 1990a.

Rural Voice, *Planning as a Creative Force*, 1990b.

Rural Voice, *Manifesto for rural England in the 90s*, 1991.

Russell, A., *The Country Parish*, SPCK, 1986.

SBBC, *Twenty Years of Shell Better Britain Campaign 1970–1990*, 1990.

SBBC, *Interactive* (the annual guide to getting help for community projects), 1995.

Scott, D., Shenton, N. & Healey, B., *Hidden Deprivation in the Countryside*, Peak Park Trust, 1991.

Scottish Office, *Scottish Rural Life*, HMSO, 1992.

Scottish Office, *Rural Scotland: People, Prosperity and Partnership*, Cm.3041, HMSO, 1995.

Shenton, N., Kirrage, G. & Scott, D., *Rural Deprivation and Voluntary Organisations and Groups*, National Council for Voluntary Organisations, 1992.

Short, B., *Imagined Country*, Routledge, 1991.

Silvester, S., The Village of the Mind, Unpublished dissertation, Cheltenham and Gloucester College of Higher Education, 1995.

Skinner, E., Patterns of Employment in Sheepscombe 1933 and 1983, Unpublished dissertation, Open University, 1983.

Skinner, E. & Howes, L., *Improving the Environment: a Guide for Town and Parish Councils*, Centre for Local Policy Studies, Cheltenham and Gloucester College of Higher Education, 1994.

Stewart, R., Indicating the Possible, *Planning Week*, 9 February 1995.

Stroud LETS, An Introduction to Stroud LETS, undated.

Suffolk ACRE, Integration of Newcomers, 1991.

Suffolk County Council Planning Department, *Strategy for Rural Communities*, 1993.

Taunton Deane Borough Council, Delegation Agreement as to Planning Functions (with Ruishton and Thornfalcon Parish Council), 1 April 1995.

Teasdale, M., Planning for People and Prosperity, in *Ruralfocus magazine*, Rural Development Commission, summer 1995.

Telecottage Association, Vital Statistics: Results of the Telecottage Survey, *Teleworker* magazine, February–March 1995.

Thomson, J.T., *Rural Futures*, University of Exeter (Agricultural Economics Unit), Report no. 243, 1995.

Thrift, N., Images of Social Change, in Hamnett, C., *Restructuring Britain: The Changing Social Scene*, Sage, 1989.

USCAN (Upton's Community Action Network), Upton St. Leonards Parish Appraisal, 1991.

Volunteer Centre UK, The Involvement of Volunteers in Rural Areas of England, Research Paper, 4, 1991.

Warburton, D., *Supporting Environmental Action*, NCVO, 1994.

Warburton, D., Mount, D. & Roome, N., *Making Community Action work in the Environment*, December 1988 Losehill Hall & SBBC Conference Report, 1989.

Welsh Office, *The Supply of School Places in Wales*, Circular 13/95, May 1995.

Welsh Office, *A Working Countryside for Wales*, Cm. 3180, HMSO, 1996.

Westminster, Duke of, *The Problems in Rural Areas*, Business in the Community, 1992.

Weyer, R. van de, *Wickwyn: A Vision of the Future*, SPCK, 1986.

Wigginton, E., *Foxfire 6*, Anchor Books, 1980.

Williams, R., Between Country and City, in Mabey, R., Clifford, S. & King, A., (eds.), *Second Nature*, 1984.

Wright, P., A Dream of England, *National Trust Magazine*, 76, 1995.

Wright, S., Rural Community Development: What Sort of Social Change, *Journal of Rural Studies* 8(1), 1992.

Young, E., Community-run shops, Unpublished undergraduate dissertation, Department of Countryside and Landscape, Cheltenham and Gloucester College of Higher Education, 1995.

Index

Short biographies
of the authors

Principal Author

James Derounian was a rural community worker in Devon (with the Rural Community Council) for six years and in Northumberland (on a local authority-led Rural Development Programme) for a further eight years. He has completed a number of rural study tours to Scandinavia, eastern Europe and other EU destinations. He is the author of *Another Country*, published in 1993 by the National Council for Voluntary Organisations (NCVO). James is currently Senior Lecturer in Countryside Planning at Cheltenham and Gloucester College of Higher Education.

Contributory Authors

Malcolm Moseley has published extensively on a range of rural community issues over many years. Formerly a Dean of Faculty at the University of East Anglia he was, most recently, Director of the national campaigning charity Action with Communities in Rural England (ACRE). Malcolm is now a Reader in Rural Community Development at Cheltenham; he also continues to serve on an 'expert committee' advising on the form and conduct of the European Union LEADER (community development) programme.

Elisabeth Skinner is a local historian and course leader of the Local Policy programmes at Cheltenham and Gloucester College of Higher Education. These independent learning courses provide training and professional development for people working with parish and town councils. Elisabeth has studied rural school-community links, and is a long-time resident of Sheepscombe, a small Cotswold village.

Rhys Taylor is a consultant on rural and environmental issues. He is a former field worker with the Community Council for Somerset. Most recently he has worked for the national charity Action with Communities in Rural England (ACRE) and headed up the Rural Action for the Environment initiative. He now lives and works in New Zealand.